Discovering
Nevada

DISCOVERING NEVADA

GARY BEDUNNAH

SALT LAKE CITY

This book is dedicated to those of the past — my parents, Pat and Neillie BeDunnah, who moved to Nevada in 1929; to those of the present — my children, Robin, Sherri, and Terri, who grew up in Nevada; and to those of the future — my grandchildren, Craig, Michael, Jordi, Ashlee, Crystal, Hannah, and Brady — for whom this book was written.

A special thanks is given for the help that my daughter Robin Swainston gave in writing this history. My colleagues George Wells and Larry Benham also contributed.

Finally, thanks to my wife, Patricia, for her suggestions and proofreading. Her encouragement made this possible.

2002   2001   2000   1999   1998   10 9 8 7

Second Edition, © 1998 by Gibbs Smith, Publisher
First Edition, © 1994 by Gibbs Smith, Publisher

Maps, graphs, and drawings © 1998 by Gibbs Smith, Publisher
Photograph credits appear at the back of the book.

All rights reserved. No part of this book may be reproduced or transmitted by any means, either mechanical or electronic, without written permission from the publisher.

Published by
Gibbs Smith, Publisher
P.O. Box 667
Layton UT 84041
(801) 547-0888 or (800) 748-5439

Cover design by Rick Sweet, Square One Design
Interior design by Mary Ellen Thompson
Cover photographs by John P. George
Editorial Director, Madge Baird

ISBN 0-87905-570-7

Contents

1. State Symbols 1
2. Nevada's Geography 13
3. Native Americans 33
4. Explorers in Nevada 51
5. Settlers and Pioneers 63
6. Mining Builds Nevada 75
7. Farming, Ranching, and the Railroad 93
8. Nevada Enters the Twentieth Century 113
9. World War II and After 131
10. Nevada's Government 145
11. Living in Modern Nevada 159

    Glossary 170
    Photo Credits 172
    Index 173

Maps and Charts

Nevada in the World 12
Nevada in the United States 14
Locating Places in the World 16
Land and Water Forms 17
Tectonic Plates 19
Great Basin 30
Historic Native Tribes 37
Native Americans Today 48
Early Exploration 60
Emigrant Trails in Nevada 72
Trails to the West 76
Railroads in the Late 1800s 109
Ethnic Population 142
Levels of Government 146
Branches of Government 147
State Revenues and Expenditures 148
How a Bill Becomes Law 151
Nevada's Counties 153
How Nevadans Are Employed 160
Gold and Silver Production 163
Products from Nevada 164
Nevada's Water Consumption 166

Sagebrush grows throughout Nevada and is a symbol of our state.

Chapter 1

STATE SYMBOLS

If you were asked to name an animal that stands for Nevada, what would you say? Could you name a flower that blooms all over the state? Do you know which tree has played an important part in our state's history? Nevada has many state **symbols**. These are plants, animals, and minerals that stand for Nevada. They show how Nevada is different from other states in the United States.

Nevada's symbols are a source of pride for the people who live here. They are also keys to understanding Nevada's history.

Nevada's State Seal

Nevada **adopted**, or took, the state seal as its first symbol. A seal is a stamp that must be placed on official state **documents**, or papers. Nevada's seal shows how Nevadans made their living in the past.

A miner and a mill stand for mining. A plow, a sheaf of grain, and a sickle stand for farming. The railroad and the telegraph line stand for transportation and communication. There are also 36 stars circling the seal. They are symbols of the 36 states that made up our nation when Nevada joined the United States. The words "All for Our Country" were added to show Nevada's support for President Abraham Lincoln during the Civil War.

The state seal shows various ways Nevadans make a living.

Nevada's first state seal had a mistake on it. The smoke from the train and the mill blew in opposite directions. As the story goes, a newspaper reporter met with the state printer. He talked the printer into drawing the seal this way. However, the reporter, Mark Twain, was playing a joke on Nevada. Mark Twain went on to become one of America's most famous writers. And Nevada's state seal was later changed. All of the smoke now blows in the same direction.

Our State Flag

Nevada's flag has been changed three different times. When the first flag was adopted, it had a blue background with 36 silver and gold stars. These stood for Nevada as the thirty-sixth state in the United States. The words *silver* and *gold* stood for our mining wealth.

Later, the flag was changed. Our state seal was placed in the center. However, the designer made a mistake. He put 37 stars on the flag instead of 36. The flag stayed that way for a long time.

Nevada's next state flag had two branches of sagebrush near the upper left-hand corner. Over the branches were the words "Battle Born." These words meant that Nevada became a state during the Civil War. In 1991, the state changed the flag one more time. On the previous flag, the letters spelling "Nevada" were placed in a circle. This was confusing. The flag was changed so "Nevada" was easier to read.

The state flag has been changed three times in Nevada's history. What do the colors silver and gold stand for?

Our State Trees

Nevada has two state trees. The first tree to be adopted by the state was the single-leaf piñon pine. It is one of the most common trees found in Nevada. It can grow in the most difficult places. Few other trees can grow in the dry, rocky ground of our deserts. For these reasons it was chosen to stand for our state.

The seed of the piñon pine is the pine nut. Early Native Americans depended on the pine nut for food. They used it in many of their dishes. Each year, they held a celebration to give thanks for the pine-nut harvest.

The piñon pine was also used by early miners. They cut the trees into timbers which helped support the walls and ceilings inside the mines. The wood was also burned in kilns to make charcoal for use in mining. Hot charcoal fires were used to **smelt**, or melt, metals from rocks.

The bristlecone pine (left) is one of Nevada's two state trees that thrive in the harshconditions here. It is one of the world's oldest living things. The other state tree is the piñon pine.

Several years ago, the bristlecone pine also became a state tree. It is one of the oldest living things on earth. Some bristlecone pines are more than 4,000 years old. Like the piñon pine, the bristlecone is also a plant that can thrive in Nevada's **harsh** land.

Our State Flower

The state flower is the sagebrush, which is really a bush that has small yellow-and-white flowers in the spring. It can grow up to 12 feet high. It grows in soil where most plants cannot. Sagebrush was used in many ways by the Native Americans. They ground the leaves for medicine and stripped its bark to weave mats.

Early settlers used the sagebrush to give them information about the soil. Where the sagebrush was tall, they knew the soil was best for growing crops.

The sagebrush was also important to animals. Cattle, sheep, and wild animals ate it during the long winter months.

The State Song

Nevada's state song was written by an **immigrant**. An immigrant is a person who came here from another country. Bertha Raffetto, while living in Reno, was asked to write and sing a song about the state for a picnic celebration. She wrote "Home Means Nevada." It describes the beauty of our deserts and mountains. It later became the state song.

The mountain bluebird is our state bird.

Nevada's State Bird

The mountain bluebird is our state bird. The male is bright blue and has a light-colored blue belly. As with most birds, the females are not as colorful. The bluebird lives mainly in the higher, cooler regions of the state. The bluebird does visit the desert floors in the winter looking for food.

Bighorn sheep are able to live in a hostile desert environment.

The State Animal

The desert bighorn sheep is Nevada's state animal. The male stands 3 feet high at the shoulder. Its large, curved horns can grow until they almost form a circle. The male weighs about 170 pounds. The female has small, spiked horns and weighs around 125 pounds. The bighorn eats grasses and the fruits of small plants.

"Old Nagah," as it was called by the Native Americans in early days, could be found all over Nevada in great numbers. However, we do not see very many bighorn sheep today. For many years, they were heavily hunted. They also had to compete with other animals for space and food. The human population was squeezing out the animal population. Finally, as people realized what was happening, they set aside areas for bighorns only. The people passed laws to protect the sheep. The sheep are now able to increase their population and live as they once did.

Nelson's Desert Bighorn, as it is officially known, is a good symbol for Nevada. It can live in our hot, dry land.

This fossil of ichthyosaur bones has been carefully uncovered from beneath the hard ground.

Nevada's Fossil, Grass, and Metal

The state **fossil** is a symbol of Nevada when the land was very different. A fossil is a print of a plant or animal of a past age. Fossils are preserved in earth or rock. Over 160 million years ago, oceans covered parts of the western United States. Animals roamed the shores and fish swam in the oceans.

One of these creatures was the ichthyosaur, a huge fish-lizard, over 50 feet long, weighing thousands of pounds. Fossils of these monsters have been found in central Nevada near the old mining town of Berlin. A state park there exhibits these fossils to tourists.

Indian rice grass grows throughout Nevada. It was eaten by early Native Americans. Desert animals grazed on it. Rice grass is a very hardy plant. It is still a favorite food for cattle and sheep.

The state metal is silver. Nevada was settled when people came looking for silver during the 1800s. Mining has played an important part in the growth of our state. While Nevada has many minerals, silver was the most important in our early mining history.

Our State Fish

Cutthroat trout are found in northern Nevada lakes. The cutthroat is a threatened species.

The Lahontan cutthroat trout is our state fish. It lives in many of west central Nevada's lakes. The biggest cutthroat ever caught in Pyramid Lake was three feet long. It weighed over 41 pounds.

The cutthroat was important to the diet of Nevada's early Native Americans. Pyramid and Walker Lakes, the Truckee, Carson, and Walker rivers, as well as Lake Tahoe, all used to have great numbers of this trout. Today, its survival is threatened because people have taken too many cutthroats from the lakes and rivers.

The State Rock

The state rock is sandstone. Sandstone was formed by a process that took over millions of years when Nevada was covered by an ocean. The layers of sand were pressed down and formed into a soft rock. This rock can be seen in Valley of Fire State Park in southern Nevada. The mountains around Lake Mead are also made of sandstone.

The idea for making sandstone our state rock came from Las Vegas school children. As a class project, they suggested to the state that sandstone be made our state rock. The government supported their suggestion and a ceremony to make sandstone the state rock was held at the Gene Ward Elementary School in Las Vegas.

Our State Gemstones

The black fire opal is the Nevada State **precious** gemstone. A precious gem is one that is rare and expensive. Virgin Valley, Nevada, is the only place in North America where the black fire opal is found.

The Nevada turquoise is a **semi-precious** gem. It is not as rare and has less value than the black fire opal. The turquoise is known as the "jewel of the desert" and is found in many parts of our state. Both stones are used in jewelry.

Many mountains in southern Nevada are composed of sandstone. This beautiful sandstone formation is in Valley of Fire State Park.

The black fire opal is the state's precious gemstone. In an opal you can see all the colors of the rainbow, depending on how the light hits the stone.

The desert tortoise, the state reptile, is now protected by law.

Nevada's State Reptile

The state reptile is the desert tortoise. The tortoise is a good symbol of Nevada because it can live on very little water. It gets most of its water from eating plants.

Like the bighorn sheep, the number of desert tortoises began to shrink. Homes were being built in areas where desert tortoises lived. Many people feared that the tortoises were becoming an **endangered species**— one that might be killed off. So the people passed laws to protect the tortoises. Any tortoises found in building sites are to be removed and taken to a protected area. It is also against the law for people to take tortoises from the desert. In these ways, the tortoises and people can live in harmony.

State Colors and Nicknames

Silver and blue are Nevada's state colors. Silver stands for our most important mineral and blue for our beautiful skies. Our state nicknames are the "Silver State," the "Battle-Born State," and the "Sagebrush State." The word *Nevada* means snow-capped in Spanish. The early Spanish traders named the region for our high, snowy mountains.

Nevada's symbols are very important to us. They show that Nevada is different from other states. Each symbol demonstrates the toughness and strength that are needed to survive in Nevada's desert surroundings. We can develop pride in Nevada by knowing our symbols and how they have made us unique.

Review Questions

1. What are symbols?
2. List Nevada's symbols.
3. What types of jobs are pictured on our state seal?
4. How many flags has Nevada had?
5. What did Bertha Raffetto do?
6. What animal was called "Old Nagah"?
7. What was the size of the ichthyosaur?
8. What do the thirty-six stars on our state flag represent?

For Thought and Discussion

9. What do Nevada's animal and plant symbols all have in common?
10. Can you suggest more symbols for our state? How could they become official?

Words to Know

symbol	immigrant	precious
adopt	smelt	semi-precious
document	fossil	endangered species
harsh		

Nevada in the World

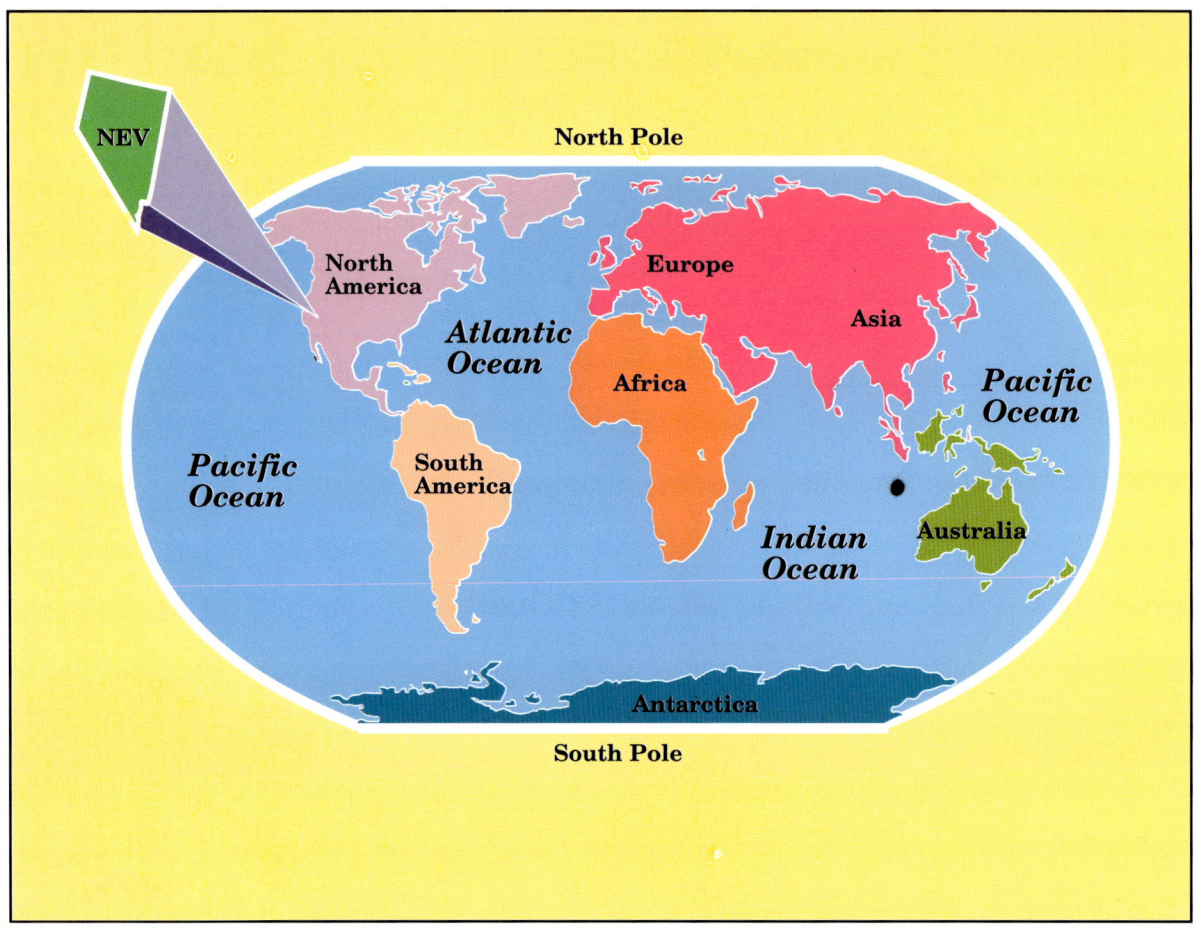

How would you describe Nevada's location in the world by using information on this map?

Chapter 2

NEVADA'S GEOGRAPHY

An airplane trip around Nevada would show you a strange and beautiful land. From above, parts of Nevada look like the movie set of an alien planet. Some rugged mountains and flat deserts appear to have no trees or plants. It seems as if nothing could or would want to live here. In other parts of the state, you see valleys covered with green farmland. There are other mountains covered with forests and grazing land stretching for miles. Small towns are few and far apart. More than anything else, Nevada is a land of contrasts. How Nevada's land was formed and changed is an interesting story.

The story begins with our geography. **Geography** is the study of the land, plant and animal life of the earth. People and the ways they change the land are also part of this science. Geography is often studied by looking at five main themes. These are location, place, relationships within place, movement, and regions.

NEVADA IN THE UNITED STATES

Location: Where in the World is Nevada?

Location explains where a place is on the earth. Nevada is a state in the western United States. Nevada is bordered by the states of Utah, Arizona, California, Oregon, and Idaho. The United States is a country on the **continent** of North America. Continents are the largest bodies of land on earth. The North American continent is part of the Northern Hemisphere. A **hemisphere** is exactly one half of the earth.

Grid System

The grid system is a set of imaginary lines drawn on maps of the earth. These lines are called **latitude** and **longitude** lines. The equator and the prime meridian are special lines in the grid system. Latitude and longitude lines cross each other at certain points. If you know the longitude and latitude of a place, you know exactly where to find it on a map. This system was invented more than a thousand years ago. A Greek astronomer named Ptolemy developed it to help travelers find their way.

Latitude lines. To help us find exact places on a map, mapmakers draw imaginary lines around the globe. The east-west lines are called lines of latitude. The equator is a special line of latitude. It circles the globe halfway between the North Pole and the South Pole.

Distance on the globe is measured in degrees. Lines of latitude measure distance above or below the equator. Lines of latitude are numbered from 0 to 90. The equator lies at 0. Latitude lines that lie north of the equator are labeled N for north. The North Pole is 90 north latitude. Those located south of the equator are labeled S for south. The South Pole is 90 south latitude. Some lines of latitude have names. The Arctic Circle is one example. It is located near the North Pole.

The equator divides the earth into two equal halves. The area between the equator and the North Pole is called the Northern Hemisphere. The area between the equator and the South Pole is the Southern Hemisphere. When one hemisphere is having winter, the other is having summer.

LOCATING PLACES IN THE WORLD

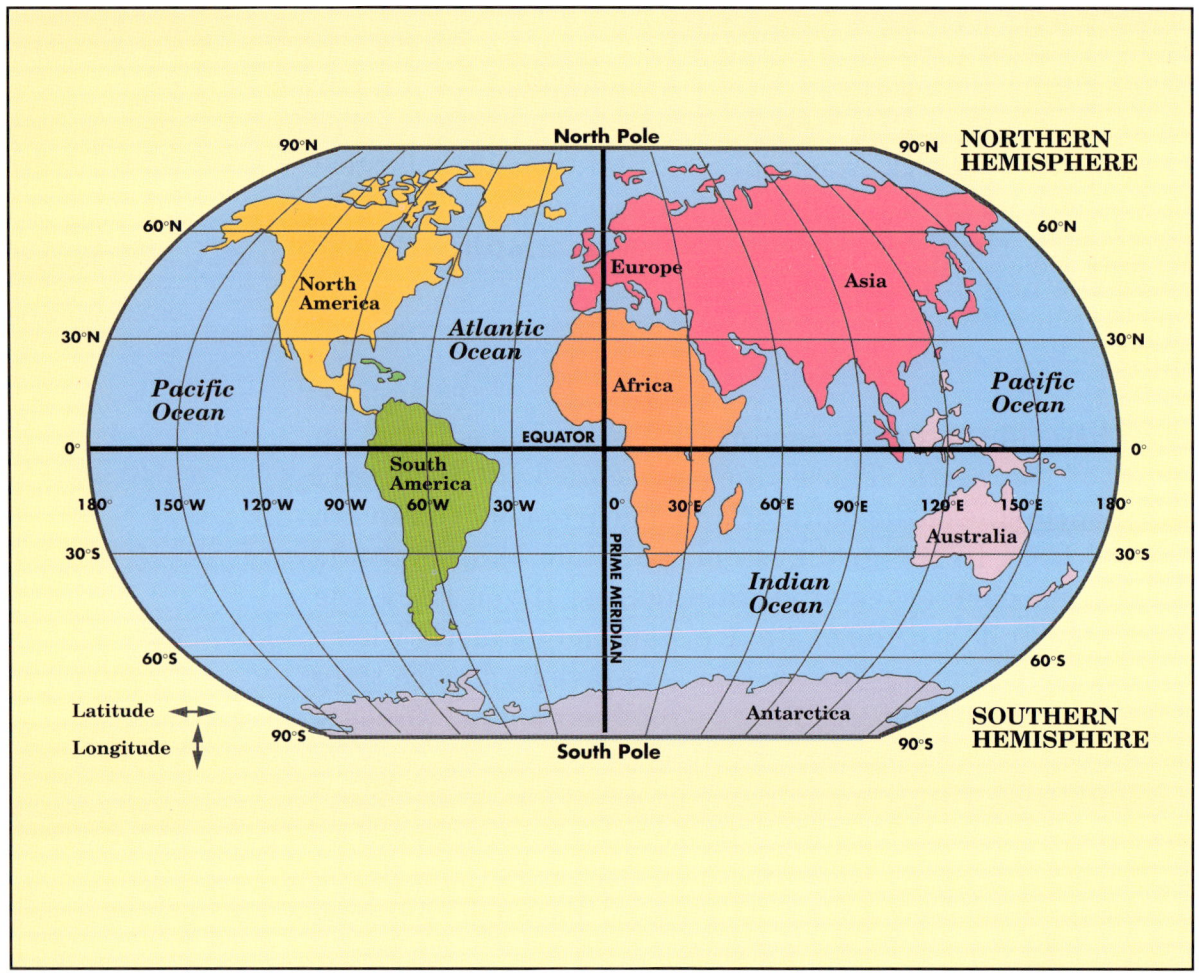

How hot or cold a place is depends partly on latitude. The farther north or south from the equator a place is, the colder it is.

Longitude lines. A second set of imaginary lines are drawn on maps to help us locate places. These are lines of longitude. Longitude lines run from the North Pole to the South Pole. Longitude lines are also called **meridians.**

The prime meridian is a special line of longitude. It runs through Greenwich, England, and is numbered 0 degrees. All other lines of longitude measure distance east or west of the prime meridian all around the earth. Lines of longitude meet at the North Pole and again at the South Pole.

Nevada lies astride lines 39 degrees north latitude and 117 degrees west longitude.

LAND AND WATER FORMS

Mapmaking

All modern maps begin as photographs. The photographs may be taken from airplanes, satellites, or spacecraft. Photographs help to make the maps more accurate. Older maps were made by mapmakers using surveying tools. Today these tools are used when the distances to be mapped are small. But when maps of large areas are needed, photographs provide better information.

Place: What Kind of Place is Nevada?

The Land

Nevada's land was formed by volcanoes, earthquakes, glaciers, water, and winds over millions of years. It has been called a land that was never finished. Rivers flow for miles and disappear into the earth. Mountains suddenly appear as if just pushed up from the earth. Rocks lie scattered as if sprinkled from the sky.

Today Nevada is a desert and mountain region. But it has not always been that way. Millions of years ago, the area we call Nevada was part of a giant ocean. As time passed, the ocean dried up. Great periods of **drought** followed, when no rain or snow fell. Volcanoes erupted, and there were many earthquakes. These caused mountains to rise. In time, the mountains were **eroded,** or worn away, by wind and rain. Then water again covered Nevada. These great weather changes occurred over a long period of time.

Nevada's **climate** changed too. Climate is the weather pattern of an area over many years. It went from being a tropical climate (hot and wet) to a desert climate (hot and dry) and back again. Many animals and sea creatures lived here. Our state reptile, the ichthyosaur, swam in the warm waters. Horselike animals, sloths, and mammoths roamed the land.

Plate Tectonics

Nevada provides a good example of nature's effects on the land. Since there is so little plant life covering the land, it is easy to see how volcanoes, earthquakes, wind, and water have scarred the earth. Why has Nevada experienced so many volcanoes and earthquakes? Scientists believe that plate tectonics holds the answer. Plate tectonics is a science that deals with the movement of the earth's crust. The earth's crust is split into many sections called plates. Each plate covers millions of square miles on the earth's surface and is many miles thick. There are two plates that affect Nevada and surrounding states. The North American and Pacific plates touch each other in

Tectonic Plates

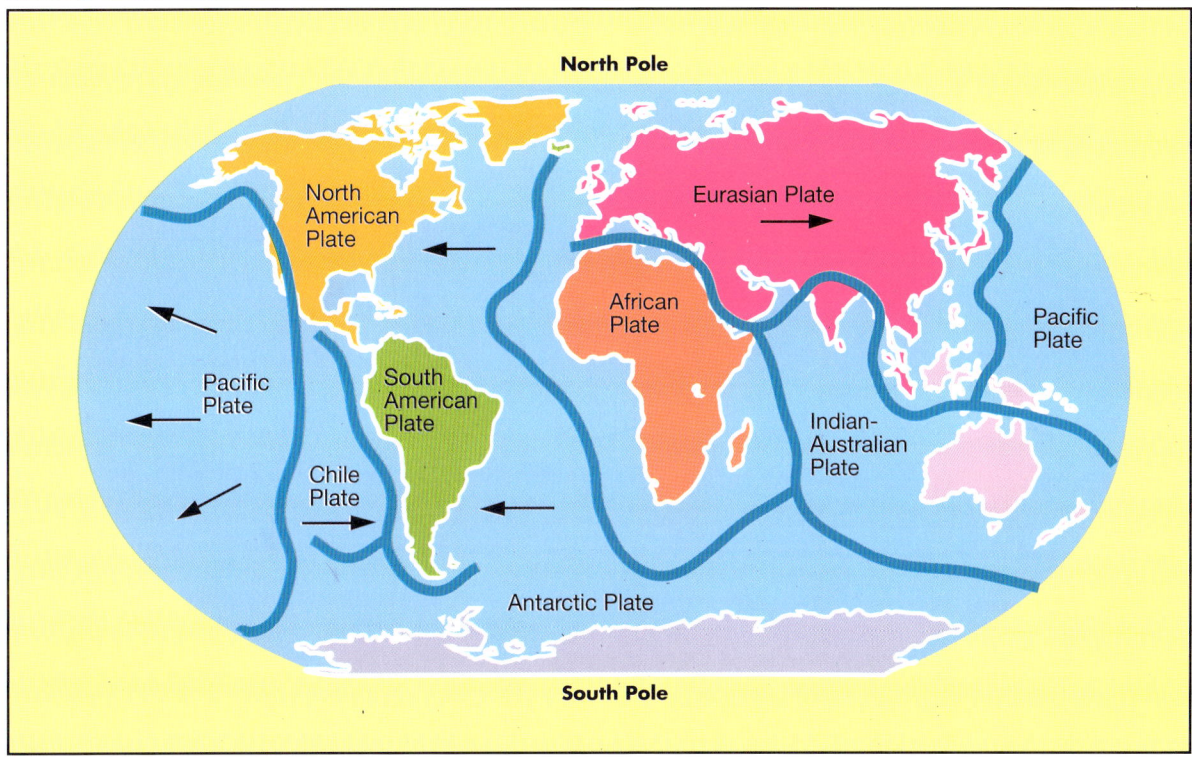

Tectonic plates move very slowly. Arrows show the direction of plate movement. Some plates are heading toward each other. Some may pass over others. Where plates touch each other is called a fault line.

several places in our region. Where they touch is called a fault line. These plates move constantly. As they do, they rub against each other. The movement and rubbing put tremendous pressure on the earth's crust. This leads to earthquakes and volcanic eruptions.

As the earth became warmer, the waters evaporated. Finally, only one large lake remained in the Nevada area. This was called Lake Lahontan. It covered much of the west-central part of Nevada. But the climate continued to become drier. Most of the prehistoric animals disappeared, because the plants they ate no longer grew. All that remained of Lake Lahontan were two smaller lakes. We know these today as Pyramid Lake and Walker Lake.

The gigantic forces of nature that have shaped Nevada left many strange and fascinating **landforms.** A landform is a feature on the earth's surface. Lehman Caves, Cathedral Gorge, and Valley of Fire are mysterious formations. They make Nevada seem like a place that has been forgotten by time.

Pyramid Lake remains today from the ancient Lake Lahontan. The large deposit of minerals is called a tufa.

Cathedral Gorge State Park shows you what water and wind can do to the land.

Landform in the Valley of Fire.

    Nature is still changing Nevada. Winds that sweep across our state carve sand and dirt from mountains and blow them from one place to another. Flash floods in the mountains wash away soil and plants and carry them to other places.

Climate becomes cooler and wetter at higher elevations, as seen here at Wheeler Peak. Trees can grow in these wet mountain regions, but not in the deserts below.

Elevation and Climate

While much of Nevada is low desert land, there are places in the state with much higher **elevations.** Elevation is the height of the land above sea level. The Sierra Nevada Mountains have a very high elevation. As elevation rises, the land, plants, and animal life change.

Temperatures and **precipitation,** or rainfall, are also quite different. The higher the elevation, the cooler and wetter the climate. The lower the elevation, the warmer and dryer the climate.

The climate of Nevada is affected by many factors. Latitude, elevation, and distances from large bodies of water are some of these.

The large, tall mountains on both sides of Nevada are part of the reason our state has a dry climate. The dry climate is due to the shadow effect. Winds blow moist air from the Pacific Ocean toward the mountains. The mountains act as barriers, preventing the moist air from reaching the other side of the mountains. As a result, very little rain or snow gets into our state.

Rain Shadow Effect

Shadow Effect

The winds from the Pacific Ocean blow clouds carrying moist air from west to east. As the moisture-filled clouds approach Nevada, they come up against the Sierra Nevada Mountains. The clouds are forced to move up the side of the mountains to get over them. As they rise, they become cooler. As they reach the top, they are cooled to the point where they can't keep their water. Water drops in the form of rain or snow on the California side of the mountains. As the clouds continue across Nevada, there is little moisture left to drop on Nevada's land.

Plants

Climate is very important in determining the kinds of plants that can grow in Nevada. Some plants can grow in dry areas, while some need more water. Plants such as the sagebrush, creosote bush, greasewood, and various cacti live in the desert regions of Nevada. In Nevada's wetter mountain regions, pines, aspen, and juniper trees are plentiful.

Sagebrush

Sagebrush grows in practically all parts of Nevada. Its root system allows it to grow on very dry land. The plant's shallow roots take advantage of rain and snow. Its deep roots get water from deep within the soil. The plant has been used by our Native Americans for clothing, medicine, and shelter. Our pioneers used it to find good soil for planting crops. It is a very tough plant that can grow to over 12 feet tall. It produces yellow flowers in season.

Mule deer. Animals, like the earliest people in Nevada, have had to adapt to the harsh climate.

Coyote.

Animals

As our land became drier and the weather hotter, the animal life changed. Smaller desert animals that we see today are snakes, tortoises, spiders, lizards, mice, desert squirrels, rabbits, and birds. The larger animals include mountain lions, bears, deer, coyotes, and bighorn sheep. Mountain lions, bear, and deer live mainly in the cooler mountain areas. Many of these animals provided food for the early people of Nevada.

Poisonous rattlesnakes are found throughout Nevada.

Rattlesnake

The Great Basin rattlesnake is one of many animals that have **adapted,** or adjusted, to Nevada's harsh climate. Because the rattlesnake cannot live in Nevada's summer sunlight for more than a few minutes, it rests in the shade during the day and hunts for food at night.

The rattlesnake is a **carnivore.** This means that it eats only meat. Its favorite foods are small rodents, lizards, and rabbits. The rattlesnake uses its tongue to smell out its **prey,** or victims.

After catching an animal, the rattlesnake uses its fangs to inject the animal with deadly poison. The snake rattles its tail when it is ready to strike. The Great Basin rattlesnake can grow to four feet in length and has diamond shapes on its back.

Where People Live and Why

Early settlers needed water for themselves and their animals. They needed suitable land on which to build towns and good soil, so they could plant crops. Because there was not much water, most settlers did not stay in Nevada. Many went to California. However, some did stay, while many others returned from the coastal states. Today, Nevada has two major **urban,** or city, areas. They are Las Vegas in the southern part of the state and Reno in the west-central part of the state. The rest of the state is made up of several small towns and farming and mining areas. Most of the state's land is still undeveloped. That means you can travel a long way and not see a town or a farm. Although a lot of people are moving into the state, it still has fewer people than most states in the United States.

Relationships: People Adapt to Their Environment

The land and climate affect how people live. People sometimes have to change the way they live if they move to a desert place with little water and no trees to build homes with. They may have to eat different food. They might have to wear different clothes.

Nevada's earliest people, the Native Americans, had to adapt to the harsh climate and limited food supply. Very little water, hot summers, cold winters, high winds, and blowing dust made living in our desert land very difficult. Nevada's Indians were not able to live as the Indians of the plains and woodlands did. They had no buffalo to hunt, and deer were scarce. They had a hard time getting food, clothing, and shelter.

Nevada's Native Americans lived on small animals, such as rabbits, and plants that grew in our deserts. They made homes from mesquite bushes and tree limbs they wove together. These early people did little to change their **environment.** They became a part of the desert in which they lived.

Many of the pioneers who later came through Nevada were headed for California or Oregon. Our desert land did not make them want to stay. Those who decided to stay here faced many hardships.

Everything that could not be made or grown here had to be brought in by horse and wagon. Most places had no trees from which to make lumber, so many homes were made out of adobe — sun-dried bricks of earth and straw. Tools, food, and clothing had to be made by hand or brought in from other places. Only those crops that required little water could be grown. Cattle and sheep could live on mountain grasses or desert plants, but they needed some water nearby, or they could not live here.

Nevada's miners faced many of the same hardships. Most miners simply wanted to get their gold or silver and leave. The land was so hard to live on, they never intended to stay. To meet their needs, the miners built towns. But places such as Virginia City and Austin required great efforts to make them livable. And when the mines stopped making money, the miners left. Many towns became ghost towns.

People Can Change the Land and Their Environment

Now, many modern conveniences, such as refrigerators, air conditioners, and heaters have been invented. Highways and railroads have been built, so trucks and trains bring in things people need. Homes and other buildings can be built with wood, brick, steel, and glass from other places. Dams and reservoirs have been built to provide a reliable source of water. It is easier to live in Nevada now. People have adapted to the climate and the land.

Movement: People, Ideas, and Goods Move In and Out of Nevada

Movement is the exchange of ideas, goods, and people from one place to another. It connects all places in some way. The gold and silver in our deserts and mountains attracted many people into Nevada. They brought with

A riverwalk has been built along the Truckee River. Visitors to Reno like to watch the water and buy food and things from the vendors who have set up outdoor shops.

them their **customs,** or accepted ways of behaving, and ideas. Men and women from many states and nations settled in Nevada's early towns. Those who left Nevada took with them the money and ideas they got here. Nevada's riches have played an important part in the development of the United States. Cities such as San Francisco, California, were built partly on the money made from Nevada mines. Mining methods developed here were used in mines around the world.

People are still coming from many places to work in the mines. And Nevada's gold and silver are now shipped to many places in the world.

Today, tourism and gambling also bring people to Nevada from all over the world. Some move here to work in these industries. Our gambling know-how is being used by other gambling centers in the nation, such as Atlantic City, New Jersey.

People, ideas, gold, silver, and many other things are always moving in and out of our state.

Region: The Great Basin

Areas of land and people that are alike in certain ways make up a **region.** A region can be small, or large enough to cover several states. In Nevada, we have mountain regions and desert regions. We have farming regions and mining regions.

Nevada and parts of her neighboring states are part of a desert region called the Great Basin. A **basin** is a low area of land surrounded by higher land, or mountains. It can have other mountains in the basin, but it is mostly flat. The states in this region are similar in other ways. Mining was an important part of their past and is still important to them. The warm winter weather of the region

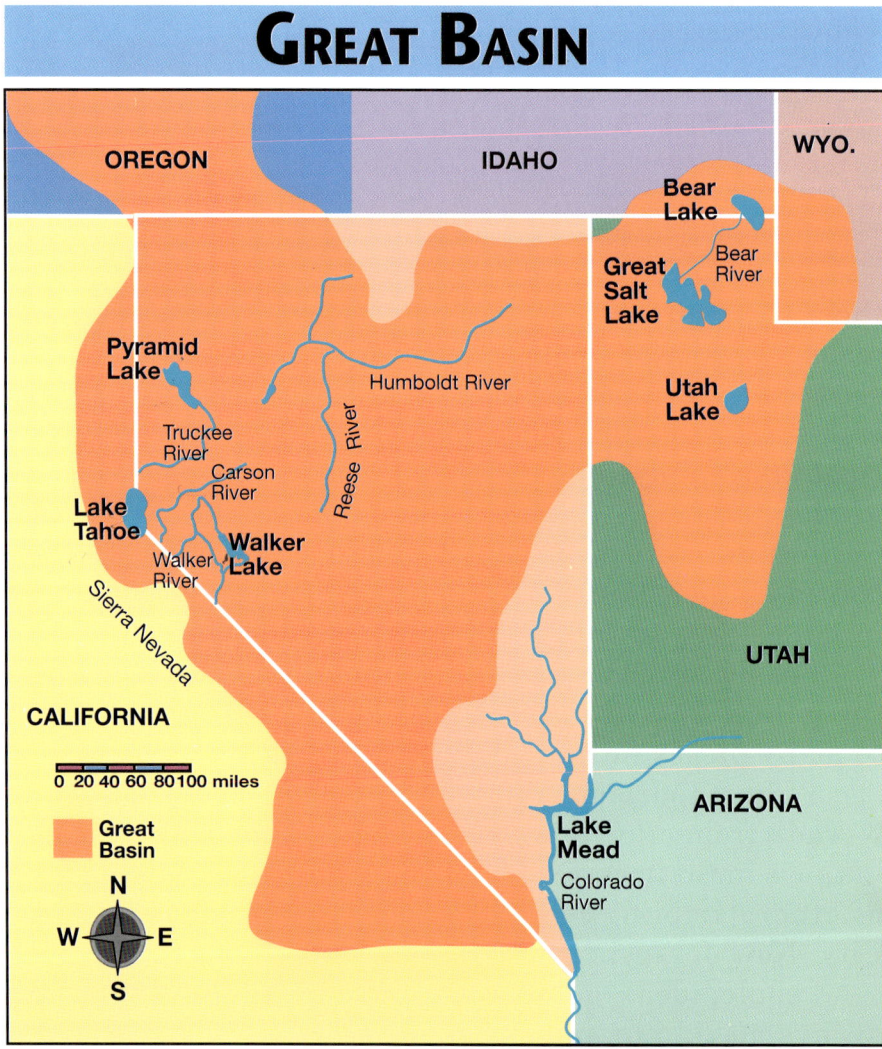

attracts vacationers and new people who want to live here. When people come on vacations or for business, they spend a lot of money on hotels, food, and gas. So tourism is a major industry of this region. Today, this region is one of the fastest-growing in the United States.

Review Questions

1. What is geography?
2. List the five themes of geography.
3. What is the geographic grid system?
4. Describe Nevada's climate changes from prehistory to now.
5. How have Nevada's land and climate affected the building of its towns?
6. How did Nevada's land determine the way early Indians lived?

For Thought and Discussion

7. How have minerals affected our state's development?
8. What does Nevada have in common with her neighboring states?
9. Explain how plate tectonics shaped Nevada's land surface.
10. Explain the shadow effect on Nevada.

Words to Know

geography	erode	prey
continent	climate	urban
hemisphere	landform	environment
latitude	elevation	movement
longitude	precipitation	customs
meridian	adapt	region
drought	carnivore	basin

Petroglyphs were carved on caves and cliffs by early Native Americans. These petroglyphs, at Valley of Fire State Park, were left by the Anasazi.

Chapter 3

NATIVE AMERICANS

Prehistoric Indians

The earliest people to reach what is now Nevada came to the region thousands of years ago. They are called **prehistoric** people because they lived before the time when written records were kept.

These people lived in caves in small family groups. **Archaeologists**, or people who study the remains of civilizations from long ago, found cave homes in a number of places in our state. Many were located near the shores of Lake Lahontan. One of these is called Lovelock Cave. Archaeologists have searched this cave for clues about the people who lived there. By studying the things they left behind, we can discover much about their way of life.

The Lovelock Cave People

Artifacts are things made by human work. Tools, weapons, and bowls are examples of artifacts. Many of the artifacts found at Lovelock Cave were made from animal bones, stone, and wood. One type of artifact found in many parts of Nevada is a stone dart point, called a Clovis point. These were attached to the ends of spears and used for hunting. The spears were thrown with the aid of a wooden tool called an atlatl. Atlatls allowed the spears to be thrown with more force and accuracy.

The Lovelock Cave people hunted ducks and other animals with their spears. Many duck decoys have been found in the cave. These were made from tule reeds that grew in the lake. The decoys were floated on the lake to attract the real ducks, which were a major source of food for the Lovelock Cave people. The people also fished, hunted rabbits, and gathered wild plants and berries.

The Lovelock Cave people spent most of their time getting food. They made clothing and other things they needed. They gathered tule reeds from the lake and wove baskets from them. They used baskets for food storage and to carry things. Remains of these baskets have been found buried in the cave floor.

We can also learn about Nevada's early people from the drawings or carvings they left on rocks and cave walls. The carvings are called **petroglyphs**. Many of these carvings are of animals. Scientists have studied the drawings to figure out their meaning. According to the scientists, the early people believed that if they carved a drawing of a deer they would be rewarded with a good hunt. Petroglyphs have been found in many places in Nevada.

The Vanishing Indians

These early people disappeared from their caves as recently as several hundred years ago. What happened to them is unclear. They left no clues to solve this mystery. Scientists have given us one explanation that seems to make sense. As the weather became warmer, Lake Lahontan began drying up. The wild animals were forced to move to find water. The early people may have followed them in order to have food.

The Anasazi Indians

Several thousand years ago, another group of people settled in the southern part of the state. They were the Anasazi. The Anasazi also built settlements in Colorado, New Mexico, Utah, and Arizona. They left many more artifacts than the Lovelock Cave people. The **ruins**, or remains, of their homes near the Virgin and Muddy rivers tell us much about their lives. There they built a large

The Anasazi built Pueblo Grande in present-day Moapa Valley.

community which is known as Pueblo Grande de Nevada, or the Lost City. This community was composed of **pit houses**, built partly underground, along with other houses built above the ground. Some houses had only one or two rooms, while others had over 100 rooms.

The Anasazi were not just hunters and gatherers. They were also farmers. They grew beans and corn in their fields. To supply their crops with water, they dug **irrigation** ditches. Irrigation is a way of supplying water to dry land through pipes, ditches, or canals. Farming allowed the Anasazi to spend more time improving their homes and lives. They did not constantly have to follow animals for food. Farming also gave them more free time to develop other skills.

The Anasazi became excellent basket weavers and pottery makers. Most of their baskets and pots were used for storage. Some were made for trade with other peoples. Pieces of these objects have been found in the ruins of Anasazi homes.

The Anasazi were Nevada's first miners. They dug turquoise and salt from the nearby hills. Salt was very important to the early people. It was used to keep dry food from spoiling. The turquoise was used to make jewelry. It was also an item to trade with other people to get things they wanted.

The Anasazi of the Lost City traded with early people in Utah and Arizona. Trade was very important to their community. It brought new items to them and helped them learn new ideas.

The Lost City Is Abandoned

About 1150, the Anasazi left their homes in the Lost City. We do not know why. They may have been forced out as a result of war with other tribes. Possibly disease or changes in the climate affected their ability to stay in Nevada. We do know there was a long dry period when crops died from too little water. The Anasazi may have had to move to find food and water.

The remains of Lost City were discovered and rediscovered several times in the 1800s and 1900s. In the late 1920s, when the building of Hoover Dam and Lake Mead was planned, scientists began to dig at Pueblo Grande. They knew that the new lake would cover up the Lost City and its buildings forever. Models of the Lost City buildings were made so that the village could be rebuilt. Today a museum near Overton shows how the Anasazi of southern Nevada lived.

Historic Indians

By the 1800s, several large Native American **tribes**, or family groups, were living in the Great Basin. Because there are written records of these people, they are called **historic**. They were not related to the Anasazi. Nor were they related to the Lovelock Cave people.

These tribes did not speak the same language. Their customs were not the same. But they did have one thing in common. All of them faced the difficult challenge of surviving on this harsh land.

HISTORIC NATIVE TRIBES

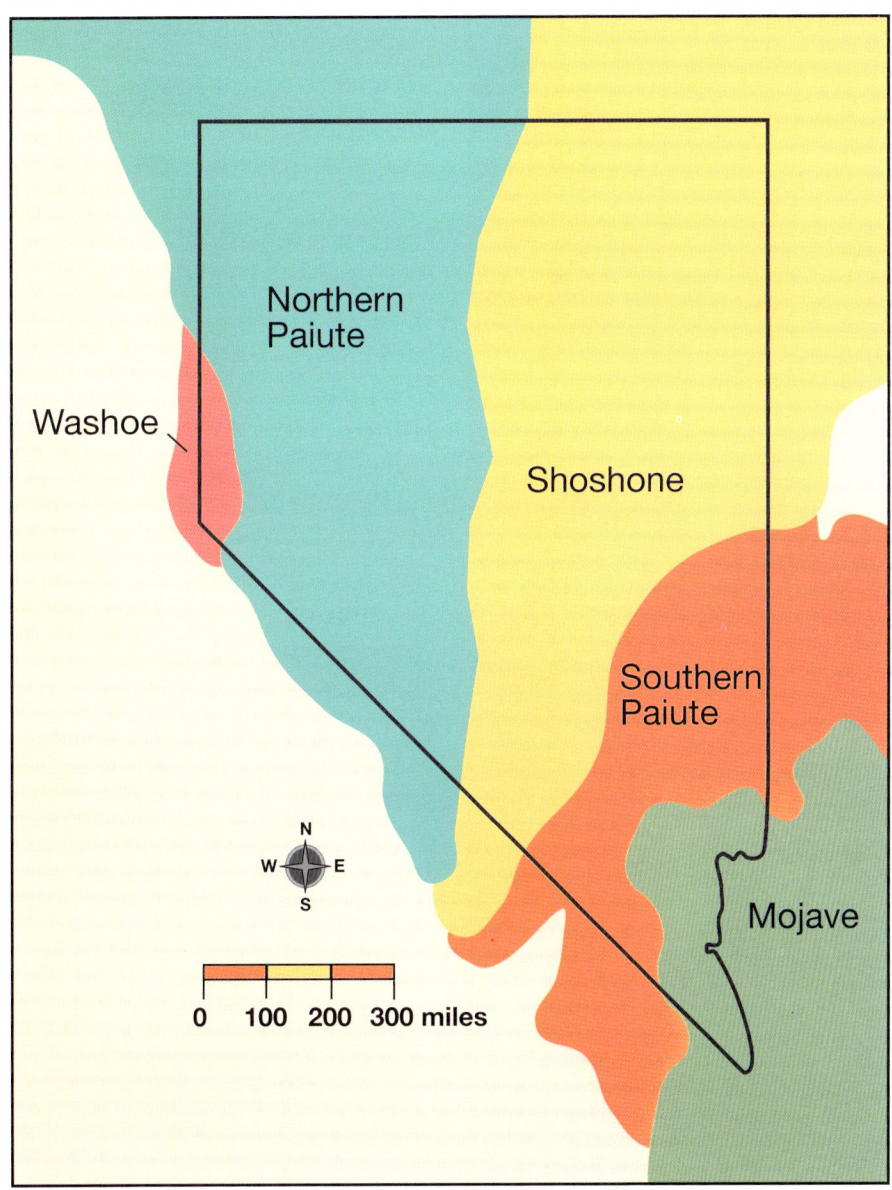

This map shows approximately where five different Native American tribes lived in Nevada during the 1800s.

Native American Life and Customs

On the whole, Nevada Indians were not farmers but hunters and gatherers. They used the natural plants in the area for their food. One of the most important sources of food was the piñon pine tree. This tree provided nuts that were used in making many foods. The pine nut became the **staple**, or main food, of the Native American diet.

Piñon Pine Nut Harvest

The piñon pine tree provided food for the early Indians. They gathered nuts from the tree in the fall. The Indians would strike the tree branches with a long pole and gather the pinecones that fell. Inside the pinecones were the nuts. The pine nuts were used in many foods. Native Americans made bread by grinding the nuts into a fine flour between two rocks. They also used the nuts in other recipes from soup to dessert. Gathering the nuts was so important to them that this harvest became a festival. It was celebrated with song and dance.

Susie Dick, Washoe Tribe, is gathering pine nuts, a staple food for Nevada tribes in the past.

Literature

The pine nut even became a part of Native American *legends*, or stories. In Washoe legend the pine nuts were at the center of a struggle between the good wolf god and the evil coyote god. According to the legend, the evil coyote god made the lives of the Washoes so bad that they were starving. To help the Washoes, the good wolf god made pine trees grow so the nuts could be used for food. But the Washoes were so weak from hunger that they could not reach the nuts on the tall pine trees. The good wolf god then made the pine trees smaller so the Washoes could reach the nuts. According to the legend, this is why the piñon pine tree is much shorter than other pines.

The Native Americans of Nevada were called "Digger Indians" by early mapmakers and explorers, because the natives were seen digging for food. Sometimes they had to eat grubs and other insects. With few animals to shoot, rabbits became a main source of meat.

Because there were no buffalo in early Nevada and only a few deer, Nevada Indians depended on rabbits for food and clothes.

Rabbit Drive

Rabbits were important to Nevada's Indians. The meat was used for food, and the skins were used for clothing. Rabbit hunts were called rabbit drives. The drives were organized by a rabbit boss. The main tool of the hunt was a large net. The drive began with all the members of the tribe in a line. They held sticks and clubs. Walking forward, the tribe beat the bushes, making as much noise as possible. The noise frightened the rabbits and made them run. The tribe chased the rabbits into a narrow canyon with no way out. Then they stretched the rabbit net across the opening of the canyon and the trap was complete. The rabbits were caught. The rabbit meat was eaten as quickly as possible before it could spoil, but some was dried and stored to eat later. The skins of the animals were made into soft, warm robes and blankets.

Indian Shelters

The homes that Nevada's Indians built had to fit the harsh climate and their wandering way of life. In the summer, they built shelters from mesquite branches. Desert breezes cooled them by blowing through the holes. In winter, the people covered poles with bark or slabs of wood to keep out the cold. These houses were simple to build. They could be left behind and new houses made with little effort. This kind of house allowed the Native Americans to move frequently during the seasons to find food.

This Paiute summer house, made simply from brush and limbs, allowed the people to move easily in search of food.

Homes made from slabs of wood kept out the winter wind.

Indian Games

The life of Native Americans was not all work. Young girls played a stick game called shinny. It was much like field hockey. They played the game with sticks and a ball stuffed with deer hair. The object of the game was to get the ball across the opposing team's goal.

Gambling games were also popular. In the hand game, someone tried to guess who was holding the animal bones. Others placed bets of rabbit skins.

The Paiutes

The Paiutes are Nevada's most well-known Indian group. They were some of the first native people whom the early explorers and settlers met up with in Nevada. At that time, most Paiutes lived together in large families, called bands.

Like other Native Americans, the Paiutes hunted small animals. They also dug roots and gathered plants, berries, nuts, and seeds for food. But Paiutes were different in one way. Some of them planted seeds and farmed. Those who lived by rivers and small streams grew corn, beans, sunflowers, wheat, gourds, squash, and melons. They cleared trees and brush to make room for farming. They even watered their crops with simple ditches from the streams. Some also fished.

At first, the Paiutes were very helpful to white explorers and settlers. The Paiutes showed the whites what animals, birds, insects, and plants they could eat. The natives taught them how to use plants for medicines. And the natives taught them to take care of the land, to farm, and to irrigate.

However, the Paiutes lived in areas of the state that the white people wanted to hunt in and live in. Because of this, there were some battles between Indians and the explorers and settlers.

Native Nevada girls played a game similar to field hockey.

These girls are wearing traditional Paiute clothing.

Famous Paiute Women

Many Nevada Indians became famous. Sarah Winnemucca was a writer and speaker for her Paiute people. She even went to Washington, D.C., to meet with the president to plead for help for the Indians. Later, she started a school for Indian children in Nevada. Her book, *Life Among The Paiutes, Their Wrongs And Claims,* tells us much about Paiute life and how the Paiutes were mistreated by whites and the American government.

Dat-so-la-lee was a famous Washoe basket maker. She made baskets during the early 1900s. She made them with such skill that they are now in museums. Today, her talents are still recognized as those of a true artist.

Sarah Winnemucca traveled to Washington, D.C., to ask for aid for her people in Nevada.

Dat-so-la-lee was one of Nevada's best basket makers.

Paiute Creation Legend

Literature

The Paiutes tell a legend about their creation. In the beginning, there was a great land between the Rocky Mountains and the Sierra Nevadas. The people who lived there were beautiful giants. They were constantly defending themselves from outsiders. One of their women gave birth to a disfigured child whom the giants treated very badly. The Great Spirit, angered by this, brought fire and lightning down on the land. The land became hot and barren. The Great Spirit also allowed the giants to be conquered by their enemies. Only two giants were left alive. The man's name was Paiute, and the woman was his wife. They were burned dark brown and made to live in a land where only a few birds could be found for food. This land was Nevada.

The Reservation Experience

In the 1860s, many of Nevada's Indians were moved to **reservations**. Reservations are sections of land set aside by the United States government where the Indians were forced to live. The old lands on which they had lived for hundreds of years were opened to white settlers.

The living conditions on reservations were often very poor. While the government provided the Native Americans on the reservation with food and clothing, it was usually too little and of poor quality. The land was not good for farming. Also, the natives' usual food—wild animals—was not available, since the Indians could not leave the reservation to hunt. Many Indians were angry that they had to live on these reservations.

Native Americans Today

Today, Nevada's Indians do not have to live on reservations. Many choose to live in towns. They work at the same jobs as other Nevadans. Some live in rural areas and own cattle ranches and farms. While our past was not always peaceful, today non-Indians and Indians live peacefully. Both know that our lives are made rich by each other's **culture**.

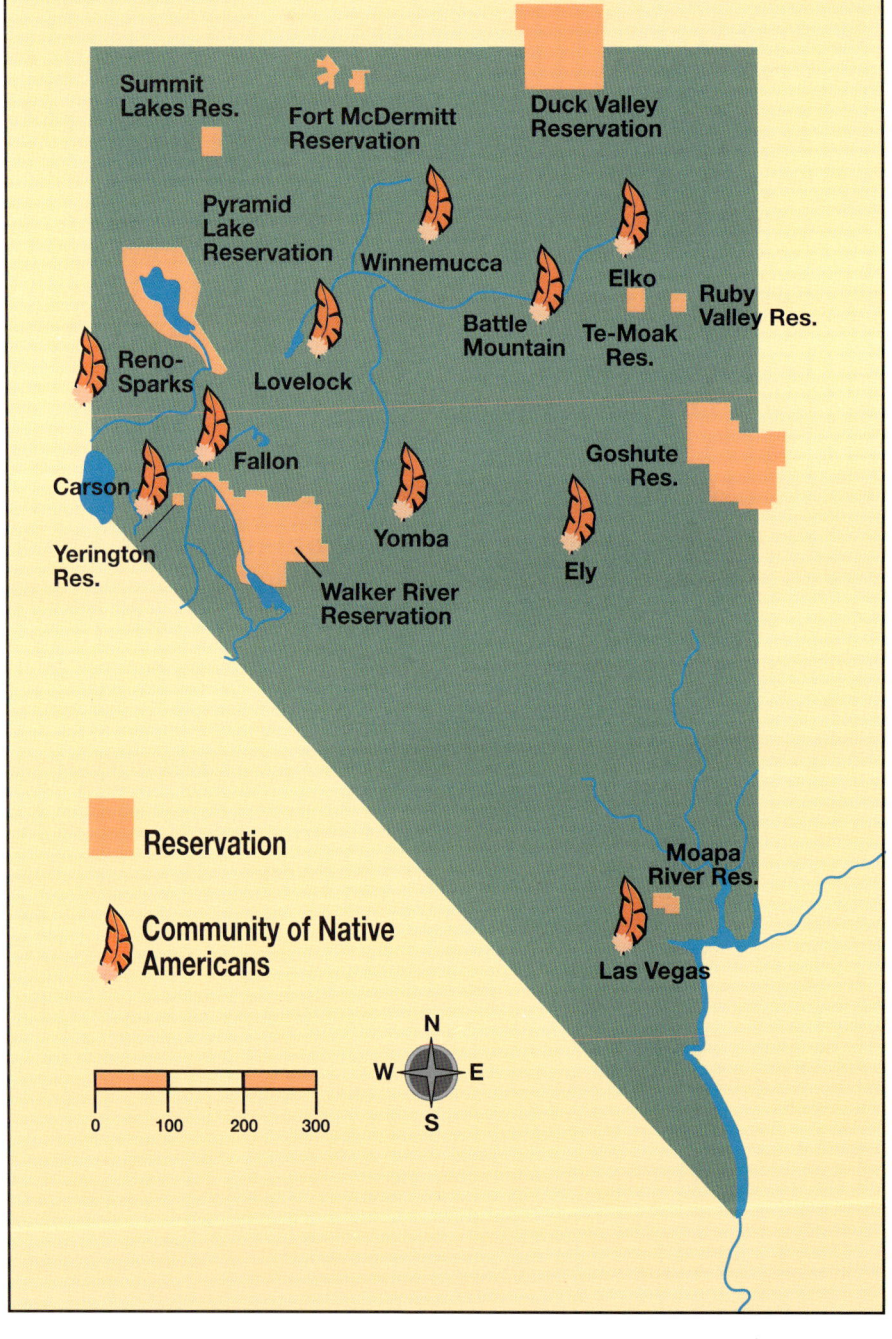

Review Questions

1. Where did many early Indians live in Nevada?
2. What are artifacts?
3. What are petroglyphs?
4. Name the early Indians who lived in southern Nevada.
5. Name the minerals that the Anasazi mined.
6. Name the tree whose nut was used for food by Nevada Indians.
7. From what were Indian homes made?

For Thought and Discussion

8. Compare the lives of Nevada Indians in the 1800s with our lives today—in clothing, homes and food.
9. Explain the Paiute legend of their creation.
10. What did Sarah Winnemucca and Dat-so-la-lee show about Nevada's Indians?

Words to Know

prehistoric	pit house	staple
archaeologist	irrigation	legend
artifact	historic	reservation
petroglyph	tribe	culture
ruin		

This painting by John Clymer shows mountain men carrying supplies by horseback. Most of the men traveled alone, but from time to time they had partners.

Chapter 4

EXPLORERS CAME TO THE WEST

By the 1770s, the western part of our country was still mostly unexplored. Spain claimed ownership of most of the region. Spanish soldiers had been sent to the American Southwest to find gold. Spain also wanted to **convert** the Native Americans to the Roman Catholic religion.

Spain had established some major settlements. Santa Fe (New Mexico) and Monterey (California) were two of these. In 1776, Spanish priests were sent to search for new routes between the two towns. Their descriptions of the land were used by map makers.

The Spanish priests traveled through parts of what are now Arizona, New Mexico, Colorado, and Utah. Since the Spaniards never entered what is now Nevada, the maps that were later drawn showing our region had many mistakes. Nevertheless, the maps were used by **traders** (people who sold goods and supplies) and others on their way to the West Coast.

San Buenaventura

Two Spanish priests named Escalante and Dominguez tried to find a river route through Utah and Nevada to California. Traveling by boat would have made the trip to California much easier and shorter. Escalante and Dominguez explored Utah and found several small rivers that they thought went into Nevada. Bad weather and lack of a guide forced them to turn back, so they did not explore the streams farther.

In their journal, the Spanish priests wrote:

Literature

> After going two leagues northwest came to a large river which we named San Buenaventura. . . . This river is the most copious [large] one we have come by. . . . Its course along here is to the west-southwest but, ahead and down to here, to the west.

Fathers Escalante and Dominguez explored the Great Basin in search of a river route to the coast. They turned back before entering present-day Nevada.

The priests thought that the San Buenaventura River went all the way from Utah to the Pacific Ocean. Even though a river that long never existed, it was important to our history. Many later explorers came into Nevada searching for this waterway.

Fur Trapping

The first explorers to enter the Nevada region were fur trappers and mountain men. In the 1700s, North America had a large and widespread beaver population. Fur trappers traveled throughout the continent searching for animals. Companies from Great Britain and the United States worked hard to see who could get the most furs.

Beavers were trapped by mountain men. Their furs were made into hats, coats, and blankets.

Beaver Skins

The animal that the trappers were looking for the most was the beaver. During the 1700s and 1800s many people in Europe and the United States wore clothing made from beaver fur. Beaver-skin hats and coats were very fashionable. Everyone wanted one.

Beavers lived in the ponds and streams throughout North America. Trappers would place their baited traps in the water. When the beavers came to get the bait, a foot would get caught in the trap. The animal would usually drown trying to get loose.

Trappers checked their traps regularly to see if there were any beavers. Trappers skinned the beavers for their fur. They took the **pelts**, which are the skins with the fur on them, to a trading post or settlement. There the trappers traded for items they needed, such as weapons, money, or food. The furs were then sent to Europe or to large cities in the United States to be made into hats and other clothing.

Many mountain men made their living by trapping beavers.

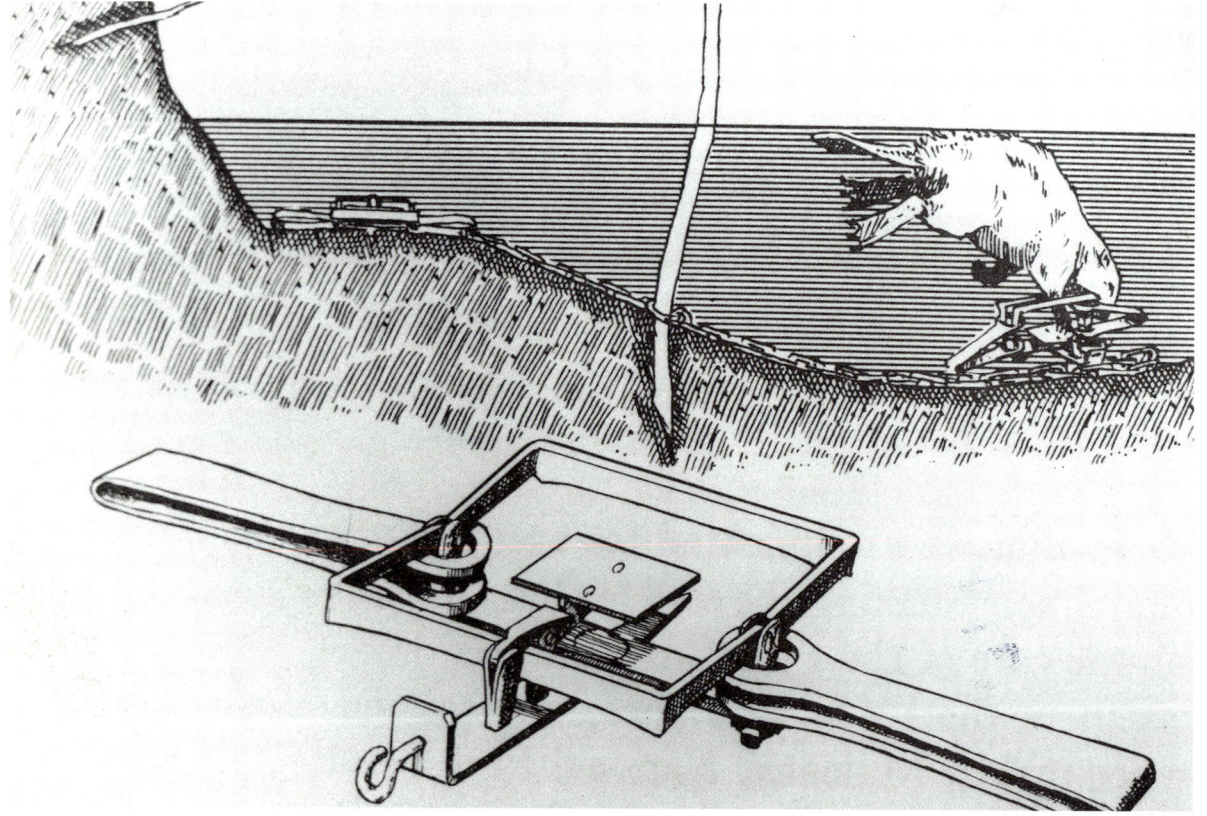

The Mountain Men

Because trappers in our western United States spent long periods of time hunting in the mountains, they became known as mountain men. These men were very rough and rugged. They had to find their own food and shelter in the mountains and deserts of the West.

The mountain men often hunted in lands where the Native Americans lived. Many Indians and mountain men became friends, and traded with each other. Some mountain men made Native American women their wives. They even joined Indian tribes. However, some Native Americans viewed the trappers as trespassers in their land. This

What does this John Clymer painting, *Night Visitors,* tell about the life of a mountain man?

led to conflicts. Battles between the mountain men and Native Americans became legends in the West.

One of these legends tells of a mountain man known as Liver Eating Johnson. His family was killed by Indians. From that time on he hunted Indians to kill. He is said to have earned his nickname by what he did to the Indians that he killed.

Literature

The mountain men also had to face wild animals, such as bears and mountain lions. According to one story, mountain man Jedediah Smith met a grizzly bear one day. In the fight that followed, the bear tore off Smith's ear before Smith was able to kill it. He then had a friend sew his ear back on. But the friend did it upside down. After that, Smith wore his hair long on one side to cover the misshapen ear.

The Rendezvous

Once each year the mountain men met with the people who bought their furs. Often friendly Native Americans came too. These meetings were called **rendezvous**. They were like long, wild parties. Games and contests were often part of these meetings. One contest was a race to see who could eat the cooked intestines of a buffalo the fastest. In another game, men shot cups of whiskey off one another's heads to prove their bravery.

Gambling games were very popular with the trappers. They would bet on anything from foot races to horse races. Sometimes they played the Indian hand game. The object of this game was to guess who was hiding a stone or bone in his hand.

Some rendezvous lasted a week. When the trappers had spent most of their money, they headed back to the mountains for another year. The rendezvous made the mountain men legends in American western history.

Mountain men looked forward to the yearly rendezvous, where they could trade their pelts for supplies and have a good time for a few days. This painting of a rendezvous is by a famous western painter, John Clymer.

Famous Mountain Men

Peter Skene Ogden came searching for beavers in the early 1820s. During his trips into Nevada, he traveled along the Humboldt River. He also explored several other streams in northern Nevada. His trip journals were read by many people who wanted to go west. Thousands of pioneering settlers followed his trails.

Jedediah Strong Smith was another famous trapper who made several trips through Nevada. Smith and his companions faced tremendous difficulties on their trips. On one trip, his men had to eat their horses when they ran out of food while crossing the desert. When the heat became too much for the explorers, they dug into the ground for relief. The information Smith gathered about the West was sent back to people in the East.

Joseph Walker led many explorations across the state looking for furs. The record of his travels was useful to later **emigrants**, or people who left one country or region to settle in another. Walker met many Native Americans on his trips. One of these encounters led to the first recorded battle between Indians and white men. A member of Walker's party, Zenas Leonard, described the battle in his journal:

Literature

James Beckwourth, a famous African American mountain man, discovered a pass through the Sierra Nevada mountains.

> We were teased until a party of 80 or 100 came forward, who appeared more saucy and bold than any others. This greatly excited Capt. Walker, . . . and he gave orders for the charge. . . . A number of our men had never been engaged in any fighting with the Indians, and were anxious to try their skill. We closed in on them and fired, leaving thirty-nine dead on the field . . . the remainder running into the highgrass in every direction.

Jim Beckwourth was one of the few mountain men who was an African American. Besides being a trapper, Beckwourth was also an army scout and ran trading posts. He eventually married a Native American and became a chief in her tribe. In his journeys, Beckwourth discovered a famous pass in the Sierra Nevadas. This pass made it easier for pioneers to get through the high mountains to California. His life is described in his own book, *Life and Adventures of James P. Beckwourth*.

John C. Fremont was the most famous explorer of our state. Fremont was an army officer. His job was to map the Southwest. He was the first to make accurate maps of this region. During his travels in Nevada, Fremont named several important lakes and rivers. He named the Humboldt River, Pyramid Lake, Walker River, and Walker Lake. He named the Great Basin too. Fremont also followed the Old Spanish Trail, a trail discovered earlier by the Spanish traders. The trail went through the Las Vegas area.

It is said that during his trip across Southern Nevada, Fremont had to leave a cannon in the mountains because of the deep snows. People still look for this cannon near the Potosi Mountains.

In his *Geographical Memoir*, a journal of his travels, Fremont wrote the following:

Literature

> **Rivers of the Great Basin. The most considerable river in the interior of the Great Basin is the one called on the map Humboldt River. . . . It is a very peculiar stream . . . rising in mountains and losing itself in a lake of its own, after a long and solitary course.**
>
> **It lies on the line of travel to California and Oregon, and is the best route now known through the Great Basin, and one traveled by emigrants.**

Early Exploration

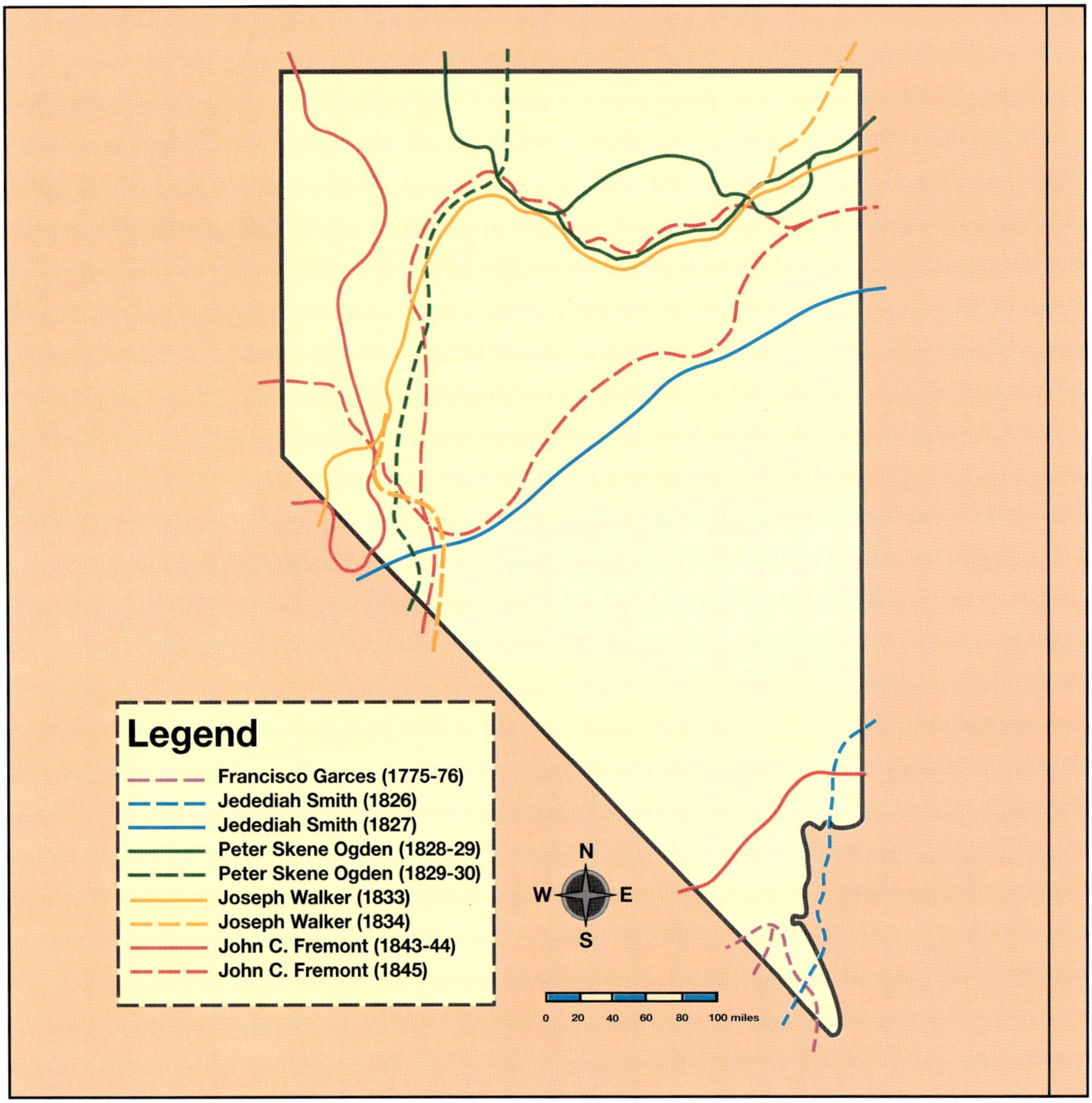

Legend
- ---- Francisco Garces (1775-76)
- ---- Jedediah Smith (1826)
- —— Jedediah Smith (1827)
- —— Peter Skene Ogden (1828-29)
- ---- Peter Skene Ogden (1829-30)
- —— Joseph Walker (1833)
- ---- Joseph Walker (1834)
- —— John C. Fremont (1843-44)
- ---- John C. Fremont (1845)

0 20 40 60 80 100 miles

Review Questions

1. Name the Spanish priests who explored our western lands.
2. What did the first explorers want in Nevada?
3. What was the annual mountain-man meeting called?
4. Who was Jedediah Smith?
5. Who was Jim Beckwourth?
6. What adventures made John C. Fremont famous?
7. What did Fremont name our section of the West?

For Thought and Discussion

8. Why did the Spanish explorers hope to find a water way through Nevada?
9. Why did the mountain men want animal furs?
10. Why were the mountain men important to the history of Nevada?

Words to Know

convert
trader
pelt
rendezvous

Traveling with the wagon train was very difficult. Not everyone could ride in the wagon. People had to take turns walking. At the end of a long day, each family fixed supper from the supplies in their wagon.

Chapter 5

SETTLERS AND PIONEERS

Many of Nevada's early **explorers** wrote about their experiences in diaries. These diaries were read by people in the eastern United States who were very excited about the adventures of the explorers. The diaries made the West seem like a promised land of great forests, rich farmland, and beautiful lakes. Many easterners became eager to travel here.

Why They Came West

In the early 1800s, most Americans lived east of the Mississippi River. Then in the 1830s, the **economy** turned bad and hard times hit the nation. Many farmers thought they would be better off if they moved to the rich lands of the West. City dwellers who were out of work believed that jobs were more plentiful out West. Some people were simply looking for adventure. Others believed that the East was becoming too crowded and wanted more space. The West had a lot of space to offer.

Pioneers came west by the thousands in trains of covered wagons pulled by oxen or mules.

How They Came West

In the 1840s, the earliest emigrants began their travels. These people were not coming to live in Nevada. It was too dry. They were going through Nevada to get to California. Emigrants traveled in **wagon trains**. Wagon trains were made up of several families traveling together. Each family loaded their wagon with their most important possessions. Clothes, furniture and food were all packed in the wagons, which were pulled by either oxen or mules. Oxen were stronger but slower than mules. Mules were stubborn. Wagon travel was very slow. On a good day, the wagons covered ten miles. At night, the pioneers arranged their wagons in a circle. It was easier to guard a group arranged in a circle than in a long line. This helped protect the pioneers and their animals from harm.

Dangers on the Trail

No one wanted to travel alone because the dangers were too great. Most of the trails were not marked with signs. The travelers had to follow directions and maps from explorers and traders that were very general. The travelers got lost fairly often. Many trails they took seemed to wander without a clear **destination**.

The pioneers often came face-to-face with wild animals. Sometimes cows and horses belonging to the emigrants were killed by bears and mountain lions. There were stories that small children who got lost had been carried off by wolves and coyotes.

Stories of unfriendly Native Americans were often **blown out of proportion**. Most of the Indians that the emigrants met were friendly. **Trade** was even carried on between the Indians and the early emigrants. Later, as more wagon trains came, some Indians began to attack the wagons. They were trying to stop the emigrants from doing any further damage to the land and animals that the Indians depended on for food. In Nevada, the Native Americans were mostly peaceful. However, there were many reports of horses and cattle being taken.

EMIGRANT DIARIES

Literature

Many of the pioneer travelers kept diaries of their trip. These writings have given us vast amounts of information about the trip, the routes, and how the people felt. An emigrant woman, Amelia Knight, wrote of meeting Indians while traveling west:

> **After looking in vain for water, we were about to give up as it was near night, when my husband came across a company of friendly Cayuse Indians about to camp, who showed him where to find water. The men and boys have driven the cattle down to water and I am waiting for water to get supper. This forenoon we bought a few potatoes from an Indian, which will be a treat for our supper.**

Emigrants had to cross long, hot, dry stretches of desert without water. Western deserts are killers, even today.

In the deserts, the intense summer heat was a problem. The worst Nevada desert that the pioneers crossed was the Forty-Mile Desert. This desert was located at the western end of the Humboldt River. The river sank into the ground there and disappeared. The wagon trains would have to cross 40 miles of desert before reaching the waters of the Carson and Walker rivers. When the emigrants saw this desert, they were bitterly disappointed. They knew they would have to empty their wagons of much of their furniture. Their oxen could not pull the heavy wagons all that way without water. Furniture of all kinds could be seen beside the trail.

During winter, the bitter cold in the mountains made travel just as difficult. For pioneers going to California, the Sierra Nevadas were the last **obstacle.** Wagons sometimes had to be taken apart so they could be lowered down the high mountains. Many people died crossing these mountains. One of the worst disasters occurred in 1846, when the Donner Party tried to cross the mountains.

These two members of the Donner party, James Frazier and Margaret Reed, plus their four children, all survived their treacherous journey.

The Donner Party

In May 1846, a group of 87 people left Missouri, headed for California. The group reached the Humboldt River by September. Within a month they were trapped by huge snow drifts in the Sierra Nevada mountains. When their food ran out, they had to eat their animals. They even ate the hides and hooves of their cattle.

One of the families in the Donner party was named Reed. Virginia Reed was 12 years old at the time. She described the horrible tale of the Donner party after she was rescued. Writing to her cousin in Illinois, Virginia said:

Literature

That same night thare was the worst storme we had that winter & if we had not come back that night we would never got back we had nothing to eat but ox hides o Mary I would cry and wish I had what you all wasted Eliza had to go to Mr. Graves cabin & we staid at Mr Breen thay had meat all the time. & we had to kill littel cash the dog & eat him we ate his entrails and feet & hide & evry thing about him.

The Donner party took the ill-advised Salt Lake cut-off across the salt desert, causing many of the delays that later led to the party's getting trapped in winter storms. Their ordeal was one of the worst ever recorded in western history.

In the final days before they were rescued, some of the trapped people ate the flesh of their dead companions. Only 47 members of the original party reached California.

Wind and blowing dust caused many pioneers to regret their decision to go west. Finding water that was fit to drink was extremely difficult. In some parts of the trail, particularly in Nevada, it was nearly impossible. The Humboldt River was the main source of water for the travelers. But it did not always run very full. In many cases, the water was foul-tasting and muddy.

Disease was another problem for the emigrants. Cholera and smallpox were sicknesses that killed many travelers. When one person contracted a disease, it spread throughout the train. There were no doctors or hospitals on the trail.

Lydia Rudd, an 1852 emigrant, wrote in her diary:

Literature

> **We passed a new made grave today . . . a man from Ohio We also met a man that was going back he had buried his Wife this morning She died from the effects of measels . . . we passed another grave to day which was made this morning the board stated that he died of cholera. He was from Indiana.**

Bidwell-Bartleson Party

In 1841, the first group of emigrants gathered in Missouri to begin their journey west to California. No one in the group had experience in leading wagons trains. No one was familiar with the land the group would be crossing. John Bartleson was chosen to be one of the team leaders. He was chosen not because of his **ability** but because he wanted to be the leader.

John Bidwell was another leader on the train. The group had no maps. They only had general descriptions from newspaper accounts. Fortunately, they were able to join with a famous explorer and trapper, Thomas "Broken Hand" Fitzpatrick. He guided them as far west as the Great Salt Lake.

From that point on, the party was on its own. They immediately ran into trouble. West of the Great Salt Lake the land is very dry and covered with salt and sand. Water was scarce. The wagons had trouble moving in the sand and they bronk down. Travel was so slow that the party broke up. Bartleson and some of the men went on ahead, while John Bidwell stayed with the rest of the he party. They traveled down Mary's River (later known as the Humboldt River). Past the Forty-Mile Desert to the Walker River they went. It took them two weeks to get through the Sierra Nevada mountains. They had to leave their wagons behind because the wagons were too heavy to get up the mountains. The entire journey took six months, but this group became the first emigrant party to cross the Great Basin into California.

Later Emigrant Parties

Other wagon trains followed the Bidwell-Bartleson trail across Nevada on the Humboldt River. But when they reached the end of the Humboldt River, the groups chose different exits from our state. Some took the Emigrant Cut-off across the Black Rock Desert into northern California, Oregon, and Washington. Others went up the Carson River into the Sierra Nevadas leading to California. Some chose the Truckee River route for their wagons. This was the route that the Donner party took.

Although the Donner party met disaster on the Truckee River route, an earlier party did not. In 1844, the Stevens-Murphy-Townsend party became the first group to get their wagons to California successfully. They were led by a mountain man who was known as "Old Greenwood." When they came to the Sierras, they had to take their wagons apart, pulling and lifting them over the mountains piece by piece.

Death Valley Trail

Many early emigrants followed the Old Spanish Trail across the southern tip of Nevada. In 1849, a group of emigrants decided to split off this trail in search of a shortcut. This group was led by Lewis Manly. Their route

took them through Death Valley, a very hot, dry desert. They nearly perished. Some of their party went ahead to get supplies. They were able to make it back to the others in time. The party struggled out of the area and gave Death Valley its name.

Settlers who intended to stay built cabins of logs. How do you think this woman felt about her cabin and living there?

Miners

Many of the people heading west were hoping to get rich in the gold mines of California. In 1848, gold nuggets had been found near John Sutter's fort on the Sacramento River. The news spread quickly throughout the United States. Thousands of people came west to find their fortune.

The main overland trail followed the Humboldt River. As these fortune hunters crossed Nevada, they looked for gold in our streams. They found some gold dust but very few nuggets.

California was said to be so rich in gold that large nuggets could be picked up off the ground. Why waste time

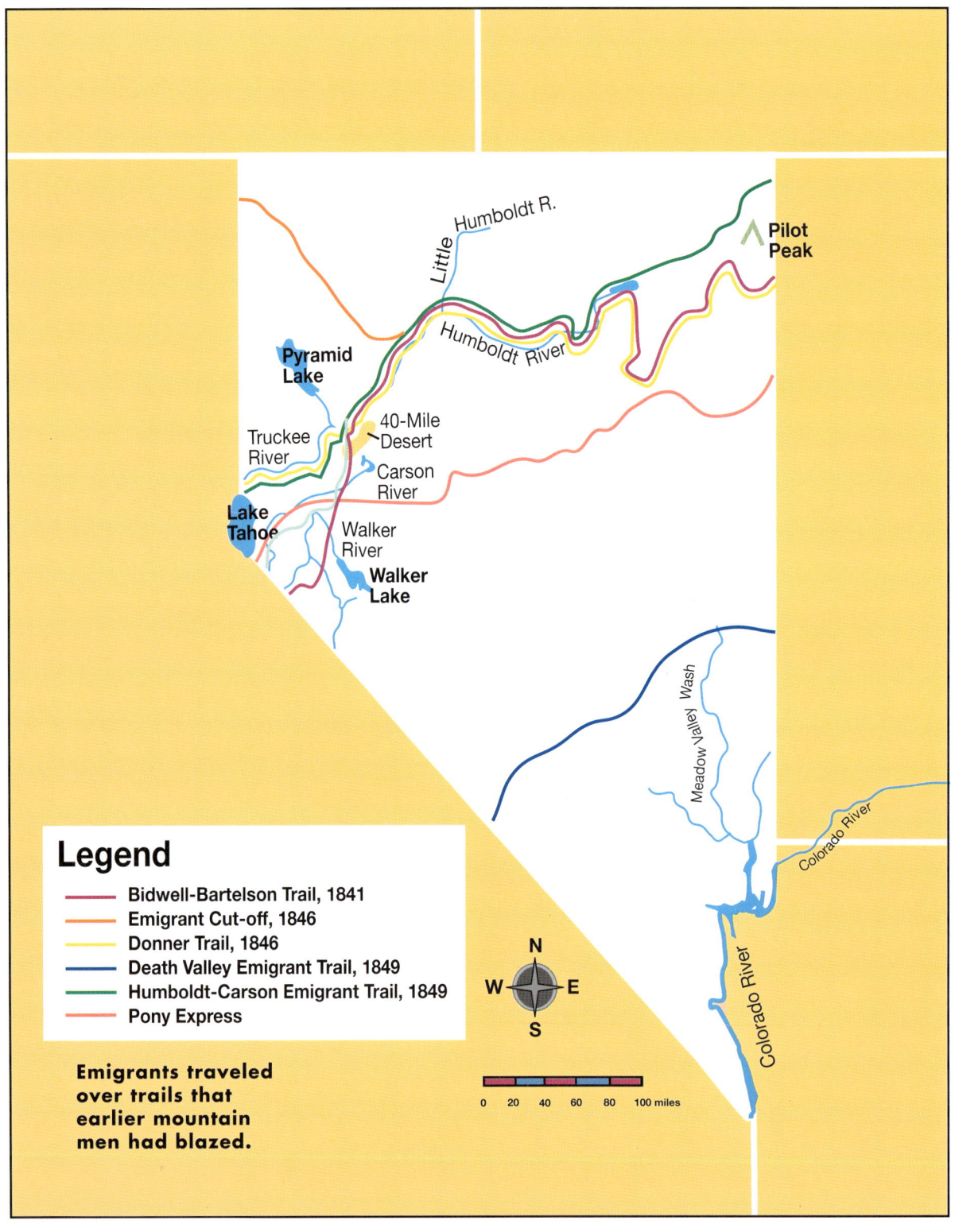

in Nevada? However, when California's gold ran out, the miners returned to Nevada to search for riches. While the early explorers, emigrants, and miners were not interested in settling in Nevada, they did make notes about the area. These records would be used by later groups who did come here to settle.

Review Questions

1. List four reasons why people moved west in the 1800s.
2. In what did the emigrant families travel overland?
3. Name seven dangers that emigrants faced in their overland travels.
4. What was the first wagon train to reach California?
5. What emigrant party was led by mountain man "Old Greenwood"?
6. What famous area in California was named by Lewis Manly?

For Thought and Discussion

7. Describe what the emigrants packed in their wagons.
8. Explain how weather was a problem to the emigrants.
9. Relate the story of the Donner Party.
10. Discuss the importance of early emigrants and settlers to the development of Nevada.

Words to Know

explorer
economy
wagon train
destination
blown out of proportion
trade
obstacle
ability

Mining was the main reason people settled in Nevada. Mining was hard work. The mines were hot and damp. Mules were used to haul heavy loads of ore from the mines. When railroads were developed, they took the place of the mules. Thousands of people moved to Nevada for jobs in mining.

Chapter 6

Mining Builds Nevada

Mormon Station was one place where travelers could buy supplies on their way west.

Nevada's First Settlement

The first permanent settlement in Nevada was a trading post. It was built at the foothills of the Sierra Nevada mountains in 1851. It was called Mormon Station. Travelers and gold seekers who were headed for California bought supplies there.

Farmers from Salt Lake City, Utah, established a settlement near the Mormon Station. It is believed that these people were the first to discover gold in Nevada. However, no one paid attention to this gold find because they thought California had a lot more gold.

People headed west along these few main trails.

Early Mining

In the early 1850s, there were some prospectors searching for minerals in an area called Gold Canyon, near the Carson River. Many of these were on their way to the California gold camps. They did not intend to stay in Gold Canyon long unless they made a big strike.

These early prospectors lived in cruel conditions. They did not build strong houses for shelter. They did not

Some miners panned for gold in streams. Others worked in dark, damp mines underground.

want to waste time building houses when they could be finding gold. They were interested only in finding their fortunes and returning home.

The miners worked from sunup to sundown on their **claims.** A claim is a piece of land legally staked out as someone's property. Miners' food was very simple: dried beans, meat from wild animals, and coffee. They were constantly getting sick from working knee-deep in near freezing waters. The miners stood in the cold rivers to pan for gold. They scooped up water, earth, and gravel from the bottom of a stream in a pan. Then they moved the pan in a circular motion. This allowed the water to slosh over the sides. After the water was all out, if the miners were lucky, there would be a gold nugget or gold dust in the bottom of the pan.

Silver Replaces Gold—The Comstock Lode

By 1859, California's gold was running out. More and more men were coming from the gold fields of California to Nevada. However, the prospectors in Nevada were not finding as much gold as they had hoped. Instead, a blue mud kept clogging up their sluice boxes, which were used to search the streams for gold. Miners threw the blue mud away. Someone had the mud inspected by experts to see if it contained any important minerals. They found that it was fabulously rich in silver ore. They had discovered the Comstock Lode.

The Comstock Lode was a huge deposit of gold and silver **ore** on the slopes of Mount Davidson. Ore is rock that contains minerals such as gold and silver.

Two men were originally given credit for discovering the Comstock Lode. They were James Finney and Henry Comstock. Finney apparently did discover gold ore, but Comstock talked his way into a partnership with two other miners who had struck a second claim. The mine that they claimed was given the name Ophir. This became the first big silver mine on the Comstock.

With the discovery of the Comstock Lode, mining began to change in Gold Canyon. The first miners had done **placer mining.** Placer mining was picking loose rocks with gold or silver in them off the ground or from streams. When the nuggets were all picked up, **hard-rock mining** began. This was a way of taking minerals from rocks within the earth.

Outcroppings, or rock formation with minerals in it and sticking above the ground, were where the silver and gold **veins** were next found. Veins of minerals followed the rock into the ground. People now had to dig deep into the earth to find the ore.

The miners needed huge equipment to dig that deep. People formed companies to buy this equipment. The companies hired many miners to go down into the mines. All of these miners needed places to live. Towns began to grow. Life became entirely different from the way it had been in the early mining camps.

Life in the Mining Towns

Virginia City and Gold Hill were two of Nevada's early mining towns. Among the many buildings in these towns were saloons and gambling houses. Drinking and betting were common forms of entertainment. The miners were paid very well for their work and spent their free time having fun. Horse races were held often in these towns. Celebrations by different nationalities were also very common. More cultured forms of entertainment were also available. Concert halls were built for singers, plays, and dancing animal acts.

Most of the miners were single men. Some came from foreign countries and sent money back home to their

Literature

J. Ross Browne was a visitor to early Virginia City. Here is what he saw:

Frame shanties, pitched together as if by accident; tents of canvas, of blankets, of brush, of potato-sacks and old shirts, with empty whisky barrels for chimneys; smoky hovels of mud and stone; coyote holes in the mountainside.... To say they [the men] were rough, muddy, unkempt and unwashed, would be but faintly expressive of their actual appearance.

families. The work was hard, and the towns were rough places to live. Because of this, early towns contained many more men than women. However, some families with children lived in these towns, so the people built schools for them.

This mining camp shows several kinds of houses. Some are tents and some are tin sheds. What other kinds of buildings do you see?

BLASTING CAPS

Life in the mining towns held its share of dangers. Children often found mining equipment lying around and played with it. Blasting caps were among the most dangerous things. They were used to set off dynamite sticks. The caps contained small amounts of blasting powder.

Dan DeQuille wrote about what sometimes happened when children played with blasting caps:

In Virginia City and Gold Hill about one boy per week, on an average, tries this experiment [scratching the end of a blasting cap], and always with the same result [an explosion]. In the two towns there must now be scores of boys who lack the ends of the thumb and first and middle fingers of their left hands.

Literature

Dangers and Inventions in the Mines

Mining the Comstock Lode presented many problems. But the problems led to inventions that would be used in mines around the world.

Square-Set Timbering

The Comstock Lode had ore bodies that were larger and deeper than any that had been found before. This made mining very difficult. To get to the ore, miners had to dig deep shafts and long tunnels. They also had to figure out how to keep the earth from caving in on them. At first the miners tried to keep the tunnels open by using log timbers up to 20 feet long. Sometimes they would bolt two together for spans up to 40 feet. Posts held up the logs across the roof of the tunnels. Because of the extreme length of the tunnels, this method did not work on the Comstock. Frequent cave-ins resulted in terrible deaths.

This drawing shows how timbers were used to build cribs inside the Comstock Mine. The cribs were strong and worked better to prevent cave-ins.

In 1860, one of the mining companies hired Philipp Deidesheimer, a German engineer, to help solve the timbering problem. Deidesheimer came up with the idea of using shorter timbers of four to six feet to build "cribs." These cribs were like cubes that could be stacked on top of each other or joined side by side. They were very strong. They could hold up the top and sides of tunnels. The cribs could also be filled with rock to make them more stable.

These square-set cribs were very successful. By 1861, all Comstock mines were using them. This new technique was later used all over the world.

There were other dangers besides caveins. Bad air, too much heat, and falling rocks brought death and injury to many miners. Old dynamite sticks left by earlier miners sometimes exploded accidentally. This caused tunnels to collapse, trapping the miners.

Dan DeQuille, a newspaper reporter, described an accident at the Chollar-Potosi mine. A miner was pulled into the mine shaft with an empty car. He fell 890 feet into the mine. The long fall ripped the man's clothing and crushed him. The miners faced such dangers every day.

Sutro Tunnel

The Comstock mines were so deep that miners reached pockets of boiling water. This water was boiling because of **thermal** activity. Naturally hot water under the earth of Mount Davidson sometimes flooded the tunnels. The miners had to close the mines to pump out the water.

A man named Adolph Sutro came up with a plan to solve the water problem. His idea was to dig a tunnel from the bottom of the mountain upward. The tunnel would join the shafts of all the mines. The water would drain out of the mines down the tunnel. It would empty out on the floor of the desert. To pay for building the tunnel, Sutro would charge the mine owners for using it. He would also provide milling service, crushing the rock to get out the silver, in his new town of Sutro.

The tunnel was completed after nine years. By that time, most of the mines were running out of ore. So the tunnel was not used much. However, the tunnel was recognized as an engineering marvel.

Personalities on the Comstock

Nevada's mining towns attracted many interesting characters. Virginia City was one of the largest communities between Denver, Colorado, and San Francisco, California. Many very famous people lived in Virginia City. Some gained fame because they made mining fortunes. Others became famous for other reasons.

James G. Fair and John Mackay were two partners in the Consolidated Virginia mine. This was one of the richest on the Comstock. Mackay built a mansions that still stands in Virginia City. His fortune was later used to help build the Mackay School of Mines at the University of Nevada in Reno.

Two authors also made Virginia City their home. Mark Twain and Dan DeQuille were reporters for the *Territorial Enterprise*. They became famous writing about the strange happenings on the Comstock Lode. Their articles were printed in newspapers throughout the United States and the world. Both men also wrote books about life on the Comstock. Thousands of people read these books and were eager to learn about frontier life.

MARK TWAIN

Mark Twain, whose real name was Samuel Clemens, is one of America's best-loved authors. His classic novels, *The Adventures of Tom Sawyer* and *The Adventures of Huckleberry Finn,* have been read by generations of young people and adults as well. Twain began his writing career on the *Territorial Enterprise,* a famous frontier newspaper. He came to Nevada to help his brother, Orion Clemens. Orion was the secretary of territory under Governor Nye, the territorial governor of Nevada in 1861.

However, Twain soon tired of this job and tried his luck at prospecting. He did not strike it rich. Twain then began his lifelong career as a writer. He described his time in Nevada in a book called *Roughing It.* This book has many interesting passages about life in Virginia City, Nevada.

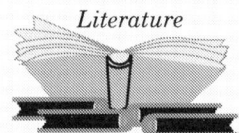

Literature

There were military companies, fire companies, brass bands, banks, hotels, theatres, . . . wide-open gambling palaces, . . . street fights, murders, inquests, riots, a whiskey mill every fifteen steps, . . . half a dozen jails . . . , and some talk of building a church.

—from *Roughing It*

Better Transportation

Transporting timber and ore to and from the mines was a problem. At first, oxen and wagons carried most of the supplies. This took a lot of time and hard work.

The building of the Virginia and Truckee Railroad solved this problem. It connected Reno with Virginia City, Gold Hill, and Carson City. It became one of the most famous short-line railroads in the West. A short-line railroad operates over a short distance.

The building of the railroad was a very difficult job. The railroad track had to go up steep mountains to reach Virginia City. Thousands of timbers were brought from the nearby Sierra Nevada mountains to build **trestles,** or bridges. These trestles allowed the trains to cross deep canyons.

This train is hauling wood for use in the mine. The train was called a "mules' relief" because it relieved the mules of the heavy job of hauling wood into the mine and dragging ore out in carts.

This trestle, or wooden bridge, carried trains across a deep canyon.

Anti-Chinese Laws

The earliest Chinese people came to Nevada to build a water ditch for irrigating farms in Carson Valley. More Chinese workers came later to build the Central Nevada Railroad and the Virginia and Truckee Railroad. Some worked in the streams trying to find gold and silver. Many employers liked Chinese workers, because they worked hard for little pay.

The miners, however, did not like the Chinese. The Chinese had different customs and a different language. Their life style was different from that of others in the mining camps. The Chinese were willing to accept lower wages for the same work. Many miners feared that the Chinese would put them out of their jobs.

Because of this fear, the other people **discriminated** against the Chinese, or treated them unfairly. The people passed laws so that Chinese could not own their own claims. They could not work in the mines. They could only take the lowest-paying jobs. The Chinese washed laundry, chopped wood, and cooked.

Sometimes anti-Chinese feelings turned violent. People burned the homes of the Chinese and beat the owners. These feelings of hatred toward the Chinese were common in California and other western states, too. In 1904, the U.S. Congress passed laws that kept more Chinese from coming to the United States.

Pony Express

Sending a letter out West during the mid-1800s took a long time. The mail went by stagecoach. It took months for a letter from the East to reach Nevada. To speed up the delivery of mail, a company started a new service in 1860, called the Pony Express.

The Pony Express hired young men to ride fast horses and carry small amounts of mail in a very short time. The company hired young men between the ages of 14 and 18 because they did not weigh very much. Then the ponies could run faster. The company also set up relay stations every 10 to 15 miles to change horses and riders. There were 29 of these stations located in Nevada.

The Pony Express operated between St. Joseph, Missouri, and Sacramento, California. The trail went across the central part of Nevada. The rider took a small mail pouch and rode as fast as he could. At each relay station, the rider traded his tired horse for a fresh one. Each rider went from 75 to 125 miles before a new rider took over. Changing riders continued until the trip of almost 2,000 miles was completed.

The Pony Express lasted only 18 months. It was put out of business by the telegraph. The telegraph sent messages over wires in an instant. The Pony Express became a part of western legend.

In this painting by William H. Jackson, a Pony Express rider trades a tired horse for a fresh one.

Camel Transportation

In the 1850s, the United States Army tested a new form of transportation in Nevada. They brought in camels to carry supplies across the desert. Camels are able to travel long distances without water. The army hoped that the camels could replace horses and oxen. Virginia City traders also were quick to try the experiment.

But a problem developed for the camels in our deserts. Nevada's desert floor was harder than that of the Sahara Desert, where the camels came from. The feet of the camels became very sore, and they refused to carry loads.

In addition, the camels frightened the horses and mules, who ran as soon as they smelled the camels.

Because of these problems, traders stopped using the camels. They turned them loose in our desert. The last of the freed camels died in the early 1900s.

Virginia City—Boom and Bust

The mines in Virginia City produced some of the richest silver deposits in the world. In the 1870s the big **bonanza,** a rich mineral strike, was discovered. Over $500 million in silver and gold was taken out of mines such as the Consolidated Virginia, the Ophir, and the Yellow Jacket.

By the end of the 1870s, most of the silver was gone. What was left was hard to get out of the rock. When it cost more to get the silver out than it could sell for, the mines closed. In Virginia City, business slowed down, and many people were out of work. People began to leave Virginia

In the middle 1800s, the mining bonanza was responsible for most of Nevada's wealth.

City to find work elsewhere. Virginia City became almost a ghost town. A few people live there today, but the town is much smaller than it once was.

Mining was the main reason people settled in Nevada. It was the chief reason Nevada became a state so quickly after it was settled. Mining was responsible for the birth of Nevada.

Beginnings of Government

The Mormon settlers of 1855 had formed early governments in Carson Valley to provide law and order. Brigham Young was the governor of Utah Territory in the 1850s. Because present-day Nevada was a part of Utah Territory, he was responsible for its citizens. He sent administrators to set up a government at the foot of the Sierra Nevadas. When Brigham Young called the Mormons to return to Salt Lake City, the only government left there was a squatter's government. This was a government formed by people who lived on land they did not own.

Later, the miners set up local governments. They wrote rules and regulations so they could feel safe while they were prospecting. But as the towns grew larger and families were brought in, the people needed more law.

The first government formed for the new settlers was a territorial government. In 1861, the president of the United States, President Buchanan, signed the **territorial government** into law. The president assigned a territorial governor to run Neveda's government. The people also voted for a few people to represent them in making laws.

Soon the people of Nevada demanded that their territory become a state. Most of the reasons for this demand involved politics. President Abraham Lincoln wanted Nevada to become a state to help him with the Civil War that was then being fought in the United States. Nevadans held a constitutional convention to set up a state. President Lincoln signed a law making Nevada a state in 1864. Carson City was named the capital of the new state. Nevada had the smallest population of all the states.

The center of Virgina City in 1878, looking east down Six Mile Canyon.

Review Questions

1. Where was the first trading post set up in Nevada?
2. What item did the earliest miners use to search for gold?
3. What was the Comstock Lode?
4. What did Phillip Deidesheimer invent?
5. What did Adolph Sutro do to help the miners?
6. What famous author of *Tom Sawyer* wrote about life in Virginia City?
7. Which president signed the bill that made Nevada a state?

For Thought and Discussion

8. How did the discovery of gold in California help bring people into Nevada?
9. What was the major difference between placer mining and hard-rock mining?
10. How did mining help Nevada become a state?

Words to Know

claim	vein	bonanza
ore	thermal	territorial government
placer mining	trestle	
outcropping	discriminate	

Nevada Territory

Legend
- Contains Nevada
- Territories
- States

Before Nevada became a state, the land was part of the Utah Territory and was govered from Salt Lake City.

Chapter 7

Farming, Ranching, and the Railroad

Carson Valley Farms

Mining gave Nevada its start, but farming and ranching helped Nevada grow too. Emigrants traveled through Nevada on their way to California and Oregon. They needed supplies on these travels. Supply stations provided the emigrants with food and equipment.

Near the Mormon Station on the eastern slope of the Sierras, farmers grew crops that the pioneers and miners needed. The farmers raised wheat, hay, barley, and vegetables. They had fruit trees plus milk cows and chickens.

Mormon Fort at Las Vegas

About the same time that the Mormons settled Carson Valley, they also started a settlement at Las Vegas. Las Vegas means "the meadows" and was named by Spanish traders who rested there on their way to California. Las Vegas had water from underground springs. There was grass for the traders' horses to eat.

In 1855, Mormon leader Brigham Young sent a group of Mormons to this well-used watering stop on the Old Spanish Trail. Young wanted them to build a fort to provide a rest station for travelers. He also wanted them to teach the local Native Americans the Mormon religion. The settlers even tried mining in the nearby mountains.

POTOSI MINE

The earliest miners in Las Vegas were looking for lead, not silver or gold. The Mormons hoped to use the lead to make their own tools and bullets. But the lead they found in the Potosi Mine was too brittle to use. This means it broke apart too easily. They soon abandoned the mine. Later, miners found silver ore in the rock, and in the 1900s, the Potosi was mined again.

The Mormon Fort at Las Vegas lasted only about three years. The settlers squabbled among themselves over who was in charge of the settlement. The Fort was abandoned when the Mormons were called back to Salt Lake City in 1858.

The Mormon lands in Las Vegas were taken over by Octavius Gass. Gass farmed the land and sold his crops to travelers. He sold the land later to Archibald and Helen Stewart. The Stewart Ranch became a famous landmark for travelers on the Old Spanish Trail.

Brigham Young sent families from Utah to build a rest station on the Old Spanish Trail. Mormon Fort was the first building in what is present-day Las Vegas.

Mormon Towns on the Colorado River

Other Mormon settlements were founded along the Virgin River and the Colorado River. These were on the present borders of Nevada, Arizona, and Utah. The farming towns of St. Thomas, St. Joseph, and the port of Callville were established here.

With plenty of river water nearby and mild winter weather, the Mormon farmers were able to grow many crops. Cotton was one of the main crops. Because of the cotton, these towns were called the Cotton Mission. The farmers sent their crops up river by boat to communities in Utah. This was a much faster way of moving crops than by land, with horses and wagons.

Riverboats on the Colorado

In the mid-1800s, riverboats steamed up and down the Colorado River, bringing supplies to mines in Eldorado Canyon. Eldorado Canyon was a mining area in southern Nevada that was undergoing a boom at that time. The boats also brought supplies from California to towns in Arizona and southern Utah. The riverboat trade lasted for over 40 years. It was replaced by the railroad.

Travel on a riverboat was very difficult. Cabins were hot and seating was very uncomfortable. There was little or no fresh food. The trip was also dangerous. Rapids made river **navigation** difficult. Large rocks, boulders, and sandbars seemed to be everywhere. But boat travel was faster than traveling overland.

Two of the riverboats were the *Gila* and the *Searchlight*. Isaac Polhamus and John Mellon were two famous riverboat captains. Their adventures made them known throughout the Southwest. On one such adventure, a riverboat entered a rapids going upstream. When it exited, the boat had turned halfway around, and the bow, or back of the boat, was facing upstream.

However, few people wanted to live in the Mormon towns along the Colorado River. They were a long way away from their families and friends in Utah. There were no other towns nearby. In time, most of the people moved away and the towns became deserted. Callville and St. Thomas were eventually covered by the waters of Lake Mead, when Hoover Dam was built. However, some of the early farm communities still exist today. Overton and Bunkerville produce farm products for people in the Las Vegas area.

Events That Helped Build Our Farm Towns

Two important events helped Nevada's farming community grow. These events were the Homestead Act of 1862 and the completion of the railroad. The Homestead Act gave free land to anyone who would spend the time and effort to farm it. This brought many settlers out west.

Water is the key to farming. Farms were established wherever streams, springs, and mountain lakes would allow. In central Nevada, farm families settled along the Carson, Truckee, Walker and Humboldt rivers, and in Paradise Valley.

These people are taking a riverboat ride for fun. Steamboats also carried food and supplies to and from the settlers in southern Nevada. Why did riverboat trade stop?

Farm Life

Life in a Nevada farm community was entirely different from that in a mining town. Farm life attracted families. Schools and churches were built to meet their needs.

Farm families worked very hard. Their day began at sunrise. They worked all day, raising crops for themselves and other people who lived in the towns. They grew wheat, corn, barley, and oats. They also grew garden vegetables such as beans, potatoes, melons, beets, squashes and cabbages. Fruits such as apples, peaches and pears were in great demand by the miners and cattle ranchers.

On a farm, everyone in the family had work to do—including the children. The larger the family, the more work they could do. Life was hard but rewarding for Nevada's early farmers.

One Nevada farmer recorded his troubles:

Literature

> **Moved into a new house. . . . But when warm weather came we were unable to sleep in the house, and were compelled to resort to the sheds and sleep on top of them to keep from scorpions, tarantulas, rattlesnakes, &, no escaping mosquitoes. [It was so hot] . . . chickens at daybreak, hold their wings up and lolling for breath. . . . An egg would roast in short time laying in the sand. I have been very much amused to see the children going home from school at noon. They would take their bonnets, aprons or some green brush (if they had them) in their hands, run as far as they could, throw them down and stand on them until their feet cooled off. Then run again. . . .**

Everyone in a farm family had to work, including the children.

Haying on Walther Ranch.

Ferris Wheel

In the late 1800s, a young boy named George Washington Gale Ferris, Jr., lived with his family on a Carson Valley farm. His family used a waterwheel to raise water up from a stream to water the farmland. It also provided water for the livestock to drink. After watching the farm's waterwheel, Ferris had a wonderful idea. He wanted to build a wheel to carry people. George designed just such a wheel and built it for the Chicago World's Fair. The ride was called a Ferris wheel, after its inventor.

The first Ferris wheel was 250 feet tall. It had 36 cages. Each cage could hold 60 people. This Ferris wheel could carry almost 2,000 people at one time. For 50 cents, a rider went around twice. The ride took almost 20 minutes. The Ferris wheel became one of the most famous rides at the fair.

Women's Rights

In 1869, a **bill,** or a proposed law, was introduced in the Nevada legislature to give women the right to vote. At this time, women throughout the nation could not vote. Men made all the laws.

Nevada legislator C. J. Hillyer, from Storey County, introduced the Nevada bill by saying, "The women of our land are human beings. They are, I presume, intelligent human beings. Moreover, sir, they are citizens of the United States."

You would think that all women would have supported this idea. But there were many who did not. Since there were so many men and women who opposed the bill, it did not become law. It would take until the twentieth century before woman **suffrage,** the right to vote in state and national elections, would be legal in Nevada.

Ranching

The earliest cattle ranches were in Carson Valley. Plenty of water and grazing land made this an ideal area for ranches. The ranchers sold beef to settlers heading to California. But the ranches really began to prosper when the Comstock silver rush began. The miners needed food for themselves and hay for their animals.

The first cattle rancher was H. N. A. Mason. Mason owned a large ranch in what is known today as Mason Valley.

Fred Dangberg started a vast ranching empire near Genoa. His family later started the town of Minden.

Ranches started in many areas of the state. In the Reese River area, ranches provided food for miners near Austin, in Lander County.

Ranches in Humboldt and Elko counties raised large herds of cattle. In the 1880s, John Sparks built a huge ranch in Elko County. Sparks brought the first Hereford cattle to Nevada. This breed of cattle provided much more beef per animal than the longhorn cattle that were raised earlier.

In White Pine and Nye counties, Jewett W. Adams and William N. McGill owned large ranches. They sold food to the miners and townspeople in those areas.

A Cowboy's Life

The life of a ranch hand was very hard work. Many cowboys worked on the ranches the year around. Some were **drifters**, men who had no home, who worked on the ranch from the spring to the fall. In the winters there was no work for them to do. Then they would have to move south to find work where the winters were warmer.

The cowboys owned very few things. Their saddles and hats were their most important possessions. In fact, many cowboys spent most of their wages on them. Their wages were low, but cowboys were given a horse, a place to sleep at the ranch, and food as part of their pay.

In the spring, the cowboys spent most of their time rounding up the cattle. During the winter, the cattle were allowed to graze freely over the ranch land to find food. Cowboys would brand the calves that had been born in the

The chuckwagon carried all the food that cowboys needed on a cattle roundup.

Literature

winter and early spring. Branding identified the ranch that owned the calves. Each ranch had a different design for its brand.

After branding, the cowboys took the cattle to places where there were good grass and water. The cows ate and got fat. This made them worth more when they were sold for beef. Then in the fall, the cowboys would round up the cattle again and take them to market.

One cowboy, William E. Abbott, told about a cattle drive:

> **We crossed the river on a boat and then we met the herd. We drove them up the river about three miles to the point where we were to swim them over. . . . We would cut out about forty or fifty head and theke them over at one time. . . . Mr. Nutter had give me a large, long stick and had me swim just above the cattle, beat them over the head and break up their milling and compel them to swim across. I did this job all day long . . . a goodly number of those steers were drowned in the river.**

Nat Love was one of the many African American cowboys who rode the western ranges.

In Nevada, many Native Americans became cowboys. There were also many African American cowboys who came from the South during and after the Civil War.

Sheepherders also came into Nevada. The earliest herds of sheep were brought through Nevada on the way to California. Richens "Uncle Dick" Wootton took 9,000 sheep across our state to the gold fields of California. In his **autobiography**, Wootton tells of the hardship of herding sheep from New Mexico:

> I knew it meant sixteen hundred miles of travel over mountain ranges, across barren plains and still more barren deserts, and in addition to this I knew that there was scarcely a mile of the road which was not beset by savages who were making it their principal business to rob and murder a white man or band of white men whenever opportunity offered.

Literature

Some herders eventually stayed in Nevada to raise their animals. They used the region's few rivers for water. Their sheep grazed on the large, open land of sagebrush and wild grasses.

Pedro Altube was a sheepherder who started a large ranch near Elko. Altube was a Basque, a person from the Pyrenees Mountains along the border of France and Spain. He brought other young Basques to Nevada. Altube paid them for their work by giving them sheep. In this way, his workers could start their own sheep ranches. Altube became known as "The Father of the Basques in America."

These ranchers are driving their cattle through a vat of chemicals to prevent disease.

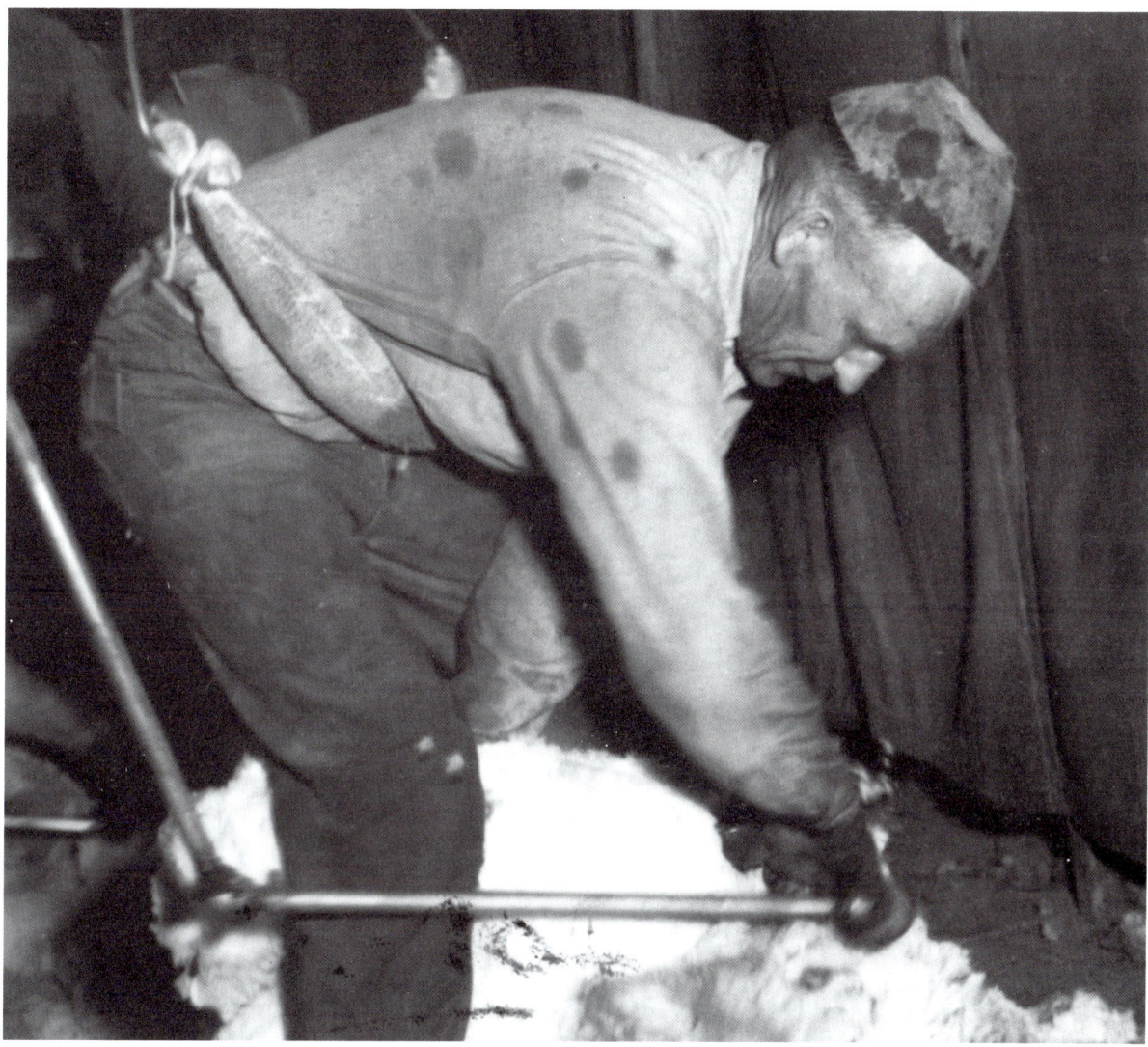

Basques

The Basque people immigrated to Nevada in large numbers between 1860 and the 1920s. The mountains of Nevada were much like the mountains of their native country.

The Basques settled near Elko, Carson City, and Ely. There they raised their herds of sheep as they had done for centuries in Europe. At first, they had problems with cattle ranchers. Cattle and sheep ranches competed with each other for control of the grassy range. But the Basques eventually became the largest **stock** producers in the state, raising animals for sale.

Basques originally came to Nevada in the late 1800s to work as sheepherders. This man is an expert sheep shearer.

At festivals Basque people dress in costumes from their native land.

Today, many people attend Basque festivals each year, celebrating the music, dance, and food of the Basque people.

The Need for Railroad Centers

The second important national event for Nevada's farming communities was the completion of the **transcontinental** railroad. This railroad linked the cities of the Eastern United States with the wide open areas of the West. It took western products back east and carried settlers out west.

The farming and ranching business grew after the railroads were built. Transporting animals and crops to market by drives and wagons was very expensive and slow. When the Central Pacific Railroad was completed,

The railroad brought many people to Nevada to build farms and to homestead the land. Can you find the route of this railroad on a map?

farmers and ranchers could quickly deliver their products and animals to the mining towns and large cities. Railroad centers were built along the route for train stops. Here people could get on and off. Things could be bought and sold. These centers became Nevada's cities.

Reno, Lovelock, Winnemucca, and Elko were major railroad centers. These railroad towns grew rapidly and still exist today.

Many short-line railroads were built to transport ore from the mines to the mills. They also brought supplies to the miners. Railroads such as the Virginia and Truckee, the Nevada Central, and the Pioche and Bullionville became very famous in our state. These railroads operated until the mines in their areas closed down. Then the trains were sold to other railroads. The rails were even ripped up and taken elsewhere.

Horses and wagons were the earliest methods of carrying supplies and people out west.

Railroads in the Late 1800s

Nevada in Decline

When silver prices fell and mining slowed down in the late 1800s, many farms and ranches began to suffer too. Farmers and ranchers no longer had anyone to buy their crops and cattle. This brought hard times to Nevada. Many people left the state to find work elsewhere. Nevada was once again a place where few people wanted to come.

This type of wooden building was common in Nevada in the 1800s. When people left the state for work, they often abandoned their homes. Some towns became deserted ghost towns.

Review Questions

1. Why was the first supply station built in Carson Valley?
2. Why were Mormons sent to set up a fort at Las Vegas?
3. Near what rivers were settlements in southern Nevada built?
4. Name two national events that brought farmers to Nevada.
5. Who owned the first cattle ranch in Nevada?
6. From where did the Basque sheepherders come?
7. Name four cities that began as railroad centers.

For Thought and Discussion

8. Describe travel on a Colorado riverboat in the 1800s.
9. Tell about the life of a farmer in a Colorado River Mormon town of the 1800s.
10. Tell about a cowboy's life in early Nevada.

Words to Know

navigation
bill
suffrage
drifter
autobiography
stock
transcontinental

Automobiles became popular in the early 1900s. At first, there were only dirt roads, but as more and more people began driving cars, roads had to be built. This photograph shows a parade on July 4, 1915, in Eureka.

Chapter 8

Nevada Enters the Twentieth Century

As the twentieth century (1900s) began in Nevada, many changes were taking place. New mining and railroad towns, new forms of transportation, gambling, better roads and schools and women's voting rights were all to become important issues.

Anne Martin

The Western states led the nation in giving women equal voting rights. The Nevada legislature heard C. J. Hillyer speak out for women's rights in 1869. But the legislature did nothing about it. It was not until 1914 that women were granted the right to vote in our state. Anne Martin was the leader of the women's movement in Nevada. As the head of the Nevada Equal Franchise Society, she traveled all over the state convincing both men and women to give women the right of suffrage. Martin later became the first woman to be nominated for the United States Senate. Martin wrote a poem to her opponent. He had threatened to leave the state if women got the right to vote:

> We'll be sorry, George to lose you
> But where are you goin' to go
> Now that the women are voting
> From Florida to Idaho?

Literature

Mining Moves South

By the year 1900, there were few mines operating in Nevada. Hard times had affected the mining industry beginning in the 1880s. Many people left the state.

However, some prospectors were still looking for riches in the deserts. Working alone, with only their burros for company, many of these prospectors were **grubstaked** by others. This meant that others paid for their supplies in return for part of any discoveries they found. Some of these prospectors made rich strikes in southern Nevada.

A Prospector's Life

Prospectors were very unusual people. A prospector sometimes spent his entire life looking for signs of gold or silver. The prospector went into the desert for months at a time. He would take very little with him in his desert travels. He packed a blanket, food and a few clothes on his burro. He took a shovel, a pick, and gun for tools.

He looked for precious metals where no one else was looking. When he found what he thought was a rich find, he went to town to **register** his claim. Some prospectors would sell their claims for a good time at the gambling saloons. Then they would head back to the desert and mountains to look for more ore.

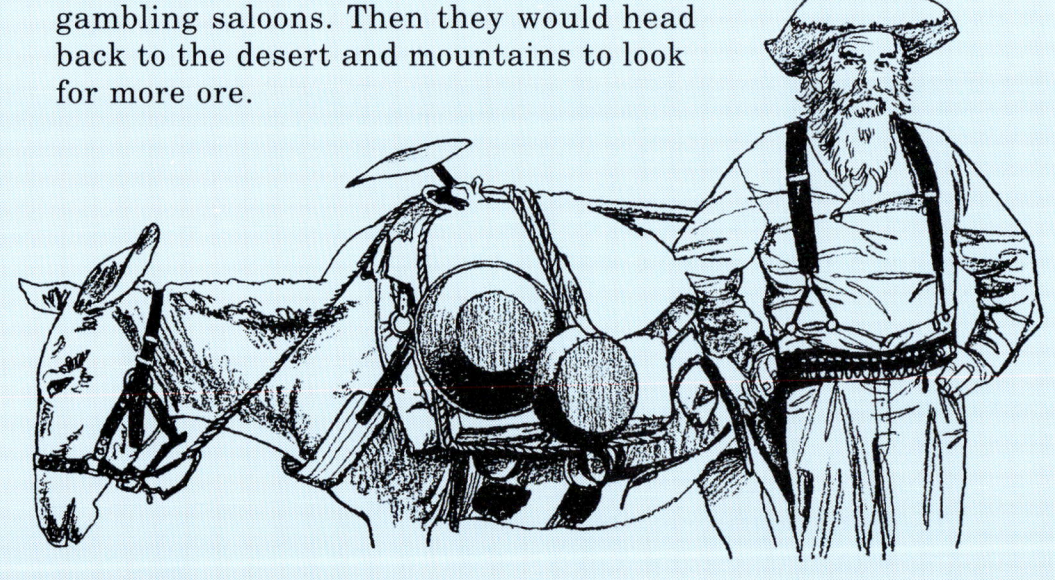

New Gold and Silver Strikes

Beginning in 1900, new mines were discovered in Tonopah and Goldfield. Mining districts with names such as Bullfrog and Rawhide helped start a new rush to Nevada.

The mining towns of the early 1900s had very **harsh** living conditions. They weren't much different from the mining towns of the 1800s. Families lived in houses that were quickly put together out of whatever could be found. Marjorie Brown described life in Tonopah in this way:

Literature

> **The problems of housekeeping on the desert were very real. During the bitter cold winters the wind moaned and whistled through the cracks in the board-and-batten houses. In the terrific summer heat, you had to cook over a wood stove with one eye always watchful for insects. . . . Have you ever turned suddenly to look at your baby on the floor and found a scorpion on his arm? Have you ever found a bedbug on your pillow and faced the task of getting rid of the pest? The women used to say that it was no disgrace to get bedbugs, but it was certainly a disgrace to keep them.**

CHAMPIONSHIP FIGHT

The new towns were very rough and rowdy. The miners enjoyed entertainment that was hard and tough, like their work.

In 1906, a championship boxing match was held in Goldfield between "Battling" Nelson and Joe Gans. It was the richest fight ever held at that time. The prize was $30,000. Gans won the fight and the money. Tex Rickard was the promoter and the fight was a great success. Newspapers all over the country described the event.

Copper in Nevada

As silver and gold were being mined in the southwestern part of the state, copper deposits were found near Ely. The huge copper pits in Ely, on the eastern side of Nevada, were worked for over 50 years. Copper was in demand because it was used in wires that carry electricity. The copper was shipped all over the world. Many people moved to Nevada to work in the pits. This metal made more money for Nevada's miners than the silver from the Comstock Lode.

Roads and Highways

The news of silver, gold, and copper strikes brought people to Nevada by the thousands. They came by horse and wagon and on foot. They also came in cars and on trains. It was a new century and new inventions were being used in this mineral rush.

In the early 1900s, railroads were still used to haul ore and supplies. Automobiles and trucks were just beginning to be used.

At this time, there were very few roads linking the new mining towns with larger cities. Cars and trucks had to be driven over the desert. This made travel very dangerous and difficult. It was also very exciting.

Horses were still useful, even after the automobile became popular.

Driving in the Desert

Travel companies advertised in local newspapers for people who wanted to have an adventure by automobile through the desert:

Literature

Go Automobiling in Death Valley with Alkali Bill. The Death Valley Chug Line runs cars daily from the Front on Borax Smith's railroad to Greenwater. Alkali Bill himself meets every train and whizzes you over the desert 45 miles by way of Death Valley and the famous Amargosa Canyon . . . in less than three hours. . . .

As more cars were used in the desert, it became clear that better roads were needed. However, the state government had little money. So they asked for volunteers to help build the roads. Finally, the state required drivers to buy licenses. The money that the government made from selling licenses was used to build roads.

These people have stopped for a picnic while driving in the desert in the early 1900s. Drivers had to be very brave to cross the harsh Nevada desert before there were roads.

Las Vegas Becomes a Major Railroad Town

Las Vegas's geographic location made it an ideal railroad stop in the desert. In 1905, the San Pedro, Los Angeles and Salt Lake Railroad was built. It connected the Utah capital city with the West Coast. Las Vegas soon became a major supply point on this new railroad.

Much of the land in and around Las Vegas was owned by Senator William Clark of Montana. He bought the land from Helen Stewart, one of the original owners of the Stewart Ranch. As head of the railroad company, Clark decided that Las Vegas would be the best place to have a supply stop because of the water there. The railroad company held an auction in May 1905 to sell lots on which stores and houses would be built. Buyers were brought in from Los Angeles and Salt Lake City on special railroad cars. This was the beginning of the town of Las Vegas.

Four years after Las Vegas got its start, it became the **county seat** of the newly formed Clark County. A county seat is the town where the government offices of the county are located.

Las Vegas became an important link to the new mining towns of Rhyolite and Bullfrog. Senator Clark built another railroad to connect Las Vegas with these new mining towns. After that, the miners received their supplies by train. They shipped the **bullion** from the mines the same way.

HELEN STEWART

Helen Stewart and her husband, Archibald, moved to their Las Vegas ranch in the 1880s. They hoped to turn it into a prosperous ranch and farm to supply travelers on the Old Spanish Trail. Two years after they arrived, Archibald was shot and killed at a neighbor's ranch. Helen was left to run the ranch on her own. She managed it, fed travelers, served as post mistress, and supplied miners in the area with food.

Helen Stewart believed in helping her fellow humans. She set up a school on the ranch for neighboring children. Today the Helen J. Stewart Elementary School in Las Vegas honors her memory.

By 1920, the new mines were running out of **ore**. The towns of Bullfrog and Rhyolite were becoming memories. Goldfield and Tonopah were barely hanging on as communities. Other mining towns, such as Searchlight and Eldorado, were being abandoned as the people left. These towns, once as prosperous as Las Vegas, were now almost ghost towns.

Las Vegas succeeded as a town because it had both the railroad and a reliable source of water. **Artesian wells**, or water flowing from the ground without a pump, and the springs of the area could support many people. Even though the town's population grew slowly in the 1920s, the town was still a major transportation stop between Los Angeles and Salt Lake City.

Las Vegas School

In the summer of 1905, the first school in Las Vegas opened. The school was held in a tent near the old Mormon Fort. By the fall of that year, however, a schoolhouse was ready. Citizens had voted to borrow money to build the school. Miss Schultz and Miss Tuttle were hired as teachers. Even in those early days, Nevada parents thought that education was very important.

Farming in the Early 1900s

Nevada's farmers and ranchers experienced good economic times in the early 1900s. In 1914, war started in Europe. Three years later the United States entered this war. It is called World War I. Foot soldiers and war machinery destroyed much of the food crops in Europe. Nevada played an important part in supplying our soldiers and the people of Europe with food.

This prize-winning steer, weighing 2,590 pounds, was raised in Ely in 1915 by a successful Latin-American rancher.

Moving Water into the Desert

The first major project of the federal government in our state was the Truckee-Carson Irrigation Project. The purpose of this project was to provide water for farming the desert regions in western and central Nevada.

Beginning in 1903, canals and ditches were dug to connect the Truckee River with the Carson River. Farmers who had been given free land by the federal government used the water that ran in these ditches. The land they had been given was dry desert land that no one wanted. But with water now available, they could grow crops. Many farmers were successful. In dry years, however, the rivers could not provide enough water to the ditches.

To store more water, the federal government built Lahontan Dam on the Carson River. The water behind the dam collected in a **reservoir**, or machine-made lake. Soon, the town of Fallon had many hundred farming families and many businesses. This federal water project was one of the first in the western United States. It was known as the Newlands Project, after Nevada Senator Francis Newlands. He was responsible for getting it funded.

Although the project did have problems along the way, it met the main goal. With water available, Nevada's desert could bloom.

Rye Patch Dam was another early federal government project in our state. A dam was built on the Humboldt River to provide water for farms in our state. The Humboldt River had long provided water for emigrants moving across our state. Now it would provide water so farms and towns could be built.

The Great Depression

The period in the world from the late 1920s to the early 1940s was called the Great Depression. People around the world were suffering from no work. In the United States as well, many businesses closed down. Banks were closed. People lost their life savings. Workers were out of jobs all across our country. People were starving because they had no money for food.

Many families lived in the deserts around Las Vegas during the depression of the 1930s.

To put people back to work, the federal government sponsored many public projects. The Hoover Dam project brought many people to southern Nevada for jobs. Homes for these people were sometimes just camps in the desert. Although the life style was not good, Hoover Dam workers earned enough to provide food for their families.

McKeeversville and Ragtown

McKeeversville and Ragtown were two early camps for Hoover Dam workers. They were made up of tents, shacks and houses in the desert. Summer heat was above 100 with no air conditioning. More than a thousand people—men, women and children—lived in these camps. Eventually, they were abandoned as the government built a new city.

The Building of Hoover Dam

Hoover Dam was built on the Colorado River. The Colorado River begins in the mountains of Colorado and flows to the Gulf of California in Mexico. It flows through Colorado, Utah, Arizona, Nevada, and California. All of these states use its water.

In 1905, the Colorado overflowed its banks. For 16 months it flooded the farmland of southern California. After the flooding stopped, a huge lake was left where

Hoover Dam supplies electricity for Southern Nevada and California.

there used to be farms. It was called the Salton Sea. People in the region asked the government to build a dam on the river to prevent such flooding from happening again.

In addition to flood control, there were other good reasons for building a dam. A dam would make it easier for boats to move on the river. A dam would store water for farms and homes. It could also be used to generate electricity. The dam's water, stored in Lake Mead, could be used for recreation.

The dam took four years to build. Between 1931 and 1935, over 3,500 people worked on the dam. Many of the workers moved here from the East because they could not find work at home.

Hoover Dam was a marvel of engineering. No one had ever built a dam as big as this before. The dam is 726 feet high and 1,244 feet long. Great amounts of concrete and steel were used in the construction. A highway crosses the top of the dam connecting Arizona with Nevada.

Hoover Dam Today

The dam uses the water of the Colorado River to turn huge generators. These generators produce electricity that is used in Nevada, California, and Arizona. The electricity is sent to these areas on lines atop large towers. The dam is also a great tourist attraction where thousands visit each year. Behind the dam, the waters of Lake Mead are used for boating, fishing, and swimming.

Boulder City

With so many people working on Hoover Dam, it became necessary to build a town to house the workers and their families. This town was Boulder City.

The government built the town and paid for everything, from houses to businesses. At first, the government **leased** the land to the residents. After the dam was completed, many people moved away to find new work. Today Boulder City attracts many people because of its small-town life style.

Gambling and Tourism

As the depression of the 1930s grew worse, the state began to run out of money to pay for needed public projects in Nevada. Highways were needed to encourage tourists to travel in our state. Dams and reservoirs were needed to provide farmers with a steady supply of water for their crops. A new source of tax money was needed. Making gambling legal and taxing it was the answer.

Gambling had long been a part of frontier town life. At times, gambling had been outlawed. But even when it was, people found ways to bet on cards, dice, horses, and sporting events.

In 1931, Nevada passed a law legalizing gambling. It became the first state in the country to do so. At first, legalized gambling did not have a big impact on the state's economy. Few people realized how important gambling would become to our state. But Nevada's location was important to its success as a gambling center. Nevada was near large population centers in California. This made it easy for Californians to come to our state to gamble. They spent a lot of money while they were here. The casinos paid taxes on their earnings. Today these taxes help pay for the schools, highways, health care, and other public services in Nevada.

Hotels and Resorts

By 1933, Las Vegas began to call itself the capital of gambling. Adults enjoyed playing cards and dice in the new casinos downtown. The Northern Club and the Silver Club were very popular. However, tourists did not come to gamble in great numbers until the 1940s. In 1941, the state's first hotel and gambling resort opened. It was located on the highway to Los Angeles. The resort was called the El Rancho Vegas. It was the start of the famous Las Vegas Strip. The El Rancho Vegas was soon joined by the Last Frontier Hotel. The most famous new hotel on the Strip, The Flamingo, was built by a the well-known criminal Benjamin "Bugsy" Siegel. Built in 1946, it set the tone for later hotels. It was big and flashy with lots of neon

Helldorado Celebration

Brahma bull riding is a popular rodeo sport.

Helldorado was a western celebration begun in 1935. Its purpose was to entertain tourists who visited Hoover Dam. After World War II, Helldorado became very popular with locals and visitors. Parades and rodeos were to celebrate the western theme of Las Vegas. The parades had floats from all the major hotels. The rodeos attracted some of the largest crowds in town. Helldorado continues today. Fairs and carnivals have been added for people of all ages to enjoy.

lights. The Flamingo and its owner made even more headlines for Las Vegas.

Reno was also becoming a gambling center. Harold's Club was the first modern casino in that city. Raymond "Pappy" Smith, its owner, tried out a new idea that changed gambling business in Nevada. He advertised his club nationwide in 1941. He put signs up around the United States and beyond. The signs told how many miles it was to Harold's Club in Reno. The signs were in unusual places such as Alaska and islands in the South Pacific Ocean. The signs became famous and were even seen in movies.

Reno's tourist industry is based on gambling and resorts.

Lake Tahoe is considered by many to be one of the most beautiful mountain lakes in the world.

Smith also attracted customers by allowing bets of pennies and nickels in his casino. He wanted to attract the average person to his casino, not just rich, professional gamblers.

Other famous casinos were built in Reno. Harrah's Hotel and Casino was built to attract customers from Northern California and the Northwest. William Harrah also built a fantastic car collection to bring tourists to Reno.

The elegant Mapes and Riverside Hotels also added glamour to the "Biggest Little City in the World."

Lake Tahoe was a tourist attraction long before gambling became legal. Its mountains and lake make it one of the most beautiful places in the world. When year-round gaming came to Lake Tahoe, many casinos were built so people could enjoy the scenery and gamble at the same time.

Today Lake Tahoe is both a summer and winter recreation area. It is known for its skiing as well as its gambling.

Gambling

Many Gambling Games were played in the early days in Nevada. Roulette was very popular. Chuck-a-luck was also played. Card games were kept very simple. When gambling was outlawed, professional gamblers controlled the games. They often cheated their customers. One way to make the games fair was to make them legal. Government agencies could then police the games.

Divorce Law Boosts Tourism

Nevada passed another law that caused many people to come and visit here. That was the divorce law. It allowed people to get quick divorces in our state. The law said that a person had to live in our state for only six weeks before being given a divorce. Other states had much longer requirements.

As a result of this law, many people came to our state to get divorces. Reno became known as the divorce capital of the world.

It was a common story for women getting a divorce in Reno to throw their wedding rings into the Truckee River. The river ran through the middle of the town. In later years, quick weddings, along with fast divorces, made Nevada the wedding and divorce center of our country.

Review Questions

1. Where were the first new Nevada mines in the early 1900s?
2. Where were large copper deposits found in Nevada?
3. What new type of transportation was used in the new mining towns?
4. What railroad led to the building of Las Vegas?
5. Name the first major project of the federal government in Nevada.
6. Name the dam built on the Humboldt River.

For Thought and Discussion

7. Explain the reason why Hoover Dam was built.
8. How did gambling help Nevada's economy?
9. What did the 1931 Nevada divorce law do?
10. Why was Las Vegas important to the mining towns of Rhyolite and Bullfrog?

Words to Know

grubstake
register
harsh
county seat
bullion
artesian well
reservoir
lease

The Thunderbird Air Force flying team has brought fame to Nevada. Their home and training base is located at Nellis Air Force Base in Clark County.

Chapter 9

WORLD WAR II AND AFTER

What Was World War II?

During the 1930s, Europe was going through the Great Depression just as the United States was. However, two European countries allowed **dictators** to take over their governments. These were Germany and Italy. They began to make war on their neighbors. Japan joined them in their war. Germany, Italy, and Japan were known as the Axis powers. By 1939, most of the world was at war.

The United States entered the war as a result of the Japanese bombing our bases in Pearl Harbor, Hawaii, in 1941. The United States joined England, France, Canada, Australia, and the Soviet Union in the fight against the Axis powers. These nations were known as the Allied powers. The war was called World War II.

The United States had to make many products quickly for the war effort. Factories began to make airplanes, tanks, bombs, ammunition, and everything else that was needed by our armies. Millions of men and women were called to serve in our army, air force, and navy. War training took place all over the United States for these people. Nevada had both training bases and war factories.

Nellis Air Force Base

In 1941, the Army Air Force needed to find a good spot to build an air base. They needed to train fighter pilots. The air force chose the area north of Las Vegas because it was far from crowded cities. It also had cloudless, sunny weather that was good for pilot training.

The air base was called the Las Vegas Army Gunnery School. Building the base helped the economy of both North Las Vegas and Las Vegas. It put over 6,000 people to work and cost over $2.5 million to build. Much of this money was spent in southern Nevada.

The gunnery school was a great success. Thousands of men graduated from its pilot courses. After World War II, there was little need for the base and the school was closed. It reopened in 1947 on a limited basis.

When the Korean War began in 1950, the school began to train pilots once again. The base was renamed Nellis Air Force Base, after William H. Nellis, a Clark County resident who had been killed in World War II.

Pilots continued to train at Nellis during the Vietnam War in the 1960s and 1970s. Today the "Home of the Fighter Pilot" still trains pilots. It is also the home of the famous Thunderbirds, the Air Force's **precision** flying team. They perform all over the world in air shows.

Thunderbird Legend

In Indian legend, the thunderbird was one of the most powerful gods. It was usually pictured as a giant hawk or eagle. It produced thunder by flapping its wings. It made lightning by opening its eyes and by throwing lightning arrows.

Because jet engines make a lot of noise and fire, Thunderbirds seemed to be the right name for the flying team.

The Native American legend of the thunderbird led to the naming of the Air Force flying team.

Other Military Bases in Nevada

The military has chosen other communities in Nevada for its bases because of the state's geographic isolation. The navy built an ammunition **depot** near the town of Hawthorne. The U.S. Navy wanted a place to store ammunition that was not near the U.S. coastline. They feared that the Japanese Air Force might be able to cross the Pacific Ocean and bomb bases near the shore. They also wanted it to be located away from where people lived, in case there was an accident.

To store the ammunition, the navy men dug holes in the desert. They lined the holes with concrete and stored the ammunition there. This project created many jobs. The towns of Fallon, Tonopah, and Reno also have had air bases near them. These bases have helped bring jobs and money to these communities.

Henderson—
The City That Began as a Factory

World War II was also responsible for creating the city of Henderson and its factories. The federal government needed more airplanes and explosives to support the war. Both were partly made from magnesium. Magnesium is a metal made from minerals found in southern Nevada. The government signed a contract with Basic Magnesium Incorporated to build a factory in the desert near Las Vegas. The government chose this area because large amounts of electricity were needed to run the factories and produce the metal. Hoover Dam supplied the electricity.

The huge plant required a large work force. The factory employed between 3,000 and 6,000 workers at various times. The factory was so large that a town had to be built nearby to house all the workers. At first, the community was known as Basic Townsite. Later, the town was formally named Henderson, in honor of Nevada's Senator Charles B. Henderson.

Black Workers at Basic Magnesium Industries

Many of the workers at Basic Magnesium were African Americans who had come from the southern states. In fact, most came from just two towns: Fordyce, Arkansas, and Tallulah, Louisiana. Few jobs were available there and wages were very low. Entire **extended families** moved here for the good wages in the Henderson factories. The black population of Las Vegas valley rose from 178 in 1940 to 4,000 by 1950.

Because of **discrimination,** the African Americans were forced to live on the west side of Las Vegas. Later, an area of Henderson called Carver Park was opened near the plants for black workers to live. Housing there was not as good as the housing built for white workers. After the war, the plants closed and many workers were laid off from their jobs. Many of the African Americans stayed in Las Vegas. Most went to work in the hotel industry.

Workers in a Henderson plant pour metal for use in the World War II effort.

A west Las Vegas home site, 1942.

When the plants closed, community leaders feared there would be no jobs for the people and everyone would move away. But the Nevada legislature bought the plants for the state. The state arranged for new companies to use the factories to produce chemicals and other products. The town continued to grow. The city that began as a factory became the **industrial** capital of Nevada.

Nevada Test Site

On January 27, 1951, the first atomic bomb was tested in the Nevada desert. Before this, the government had done its atomic testing in the Pacific Ocean. They wanted to find some place closer to the United States to make testing easier and cheaper.

Nationwide surveys were conducted to pick a suitable location. The factors that were considered were: (1) a small population, (2) good weather, (3) a good work force, (4) government-owned land, and (5) a secure place. The Las Vegas Bombing and Gunnery Range fit the requirements. Las Vegas officials believed the test site would be good for the community. They supported the decision to build it.

In the early years, testing was done in secret. However, Las Vegans could feel the earth and buildings shake when the bombs were set off. In 1952, tests were made public. News reporters were invited to watch the explosions. Movies were made about the effects of radiation on people and animals such as the *Amazing Colossal Man* and *Them*.

Test Ban Treaty

From 1951 to 1963, hundreds of atomic tests were conducted by the United States and the Soviet Union. Many people were concerned about the amount of radiation these tests released into the air. At the same time, other nations had developed nuclear weapons and were becoming atomic powers. The nations of the world realized that the atomic testing might be harming the earth and its people. Testing equipment was developed that could detect any atomic explosions above the ground. Then the nations of the world agreed to a test **ban** above the ground. Under the terms of the **treaty**, atomic explosions are permitted under the ground. These tests are still being done at the Nevada Test Site. By the end of 1991, 714 bombs had been tested at the Nevada site.

The atomic bomb blast lit up the night sky in southern Nevada many times during the 1950s and 1960s.

Atomic Fallout Trials

The atomic bombs that were exploded above ground at the Nevada Test Site produced large clouds of radioactive dust and sand, or **fallout**. These clouds blew east over many small communities and towns in southern Utah. As the radioactive particles fell to the earth, they came in contact with the land, animals, and people.

The people in these towns were not warned of any danger from the fallout. They say the fallout has caused diseases. Their cancer rates are unusually high, and many people in this area of Utah have died from cancer. People have sued the federal government for its actions. However, it is hard to prove what caused these cancers. The issue is still being settled.

The Nevada Test Site is a major employer in southern Nevada. Thousands of workers and their families have moved to Clark County because of the job opportunities at the site. Most of the tests at the site involved military weapons. But some of the atomic devices tested have had peaceful uses. They have increased our knowledge of rocketry, well drilling, and earth removal for construction of dams.

Nevada After World War II

Nevada was undergoing changes in other areas besides politics and war. As usual, the **rural**, or farm, areas remained rather **stable**. But the urban areas were attracting new people and ideas.

In Las Vegas, the southern branch of the University of Nevada was formed. Located near the edge of town at that time, it would grow into what is today Nevada's largest university, the University of Nevada, Las Vegas.

Growth also was changing everyday life in Reno. As in Las Vegas, gaming and tourism were making that change. As new people moved to Reno, there was a demand for more parks, recreation areas, and cultural and educational events. The University of Nevada at Reno helped answer these demands. It provided leadership for the community and the entire area. The building of a unique **planetarium** and Nevada's only medical school provided services for the entire state.

Beginning in the 1970s and continuing into the 1980s and 1990s, a new boom hit Nevada. It was based not on mining but on gambling and tourism. Nevada was becoming more and more popular with people around the world.

Hispanic Americans have played a big part in making Nevada's ranches successful. Much of the language and methods for ranching comes from the Hispanic tradition. This 1913 picture shows a group of cowboys who were organized as Garcia's Elko Rodeo. Can you spot the one woman in the group?

Nevada's Ethnic Minorities

Beginning in its mining boom days, the population of Nevada has been composed of many **ethnic** groups. Ethnic groups are people from different countries or cultures. During the frontier days, Virginia City and other Nevada mining towns were settled by people from England, Germany, Ireland, Mexico, plus many other countries of the world.

Most of these people were accepted into the western society. But there were a few groups that were not accepted. We have discussed in earlier chapters about the harmful treatment of the Indians and the Chinese. In the early years of 1900, the migration of Japanese into Nevada was also viewed with suspicion by others. During World War II, because we were at war with Japan, this distrust carried on.

Wendell Williams, Nevada state assemblyman.

After World War II, many minority groups in America began to demand equal rights under the law. In Nevada, the United Paiutes, the Western Shoshone Nation, and the Inter-Tribal Council of Nevada had helped Native Americans achieve more **independence** and political influence. In many Nevada school districts, new studies about the importance of Native Americans were being used. In 1991, the state legislature made Nevada Indian Day a law.

Dario Herrera is the youngest Hispanic legislator in the United States. He works in the Nevada state legislature to get laws passed that will be good for the people he represents.

Cheryl Lau was elected Secretary of State in 1990. The Secretary of State oversees all state elections and has a role in seeing that businesses operate legally.

For African Americans, equal job opportunities and open housing were the goals. In 1961, a Commission on Equal Rights of Citizens was created in the state. It was to investigate claims of discrimination. In 1965, a law was passed that made it illegal to discriminate on the basis of race or religion in employment. African American leaders in our state, such as Woodrow Wilson in Las Vegas and Eddie Scott in Reno, became important in the fight for equal rights. Woodrow Wilson was the first black in the legislature. Eddie Scott was a leader in the National Association for the Advancement of Colored People. Today African American legislators such as Wendell Williams, Morse Arberry, and Joe Neal are contributors in the field of **civil rights.**

Asians have also benefited from the civil rights activism of the 1960s and 1970s. The Nevada Commission on Equal Rights of Citizens, in the 1960s, did not find any pattern of discrimination against Asians. Asians have made many contributions to our state beginning with the building of the Central Pacific Railroad in the 1800s. In 1981, Lilly Fong of Las Vegas was on the University of Nevada's board of regents. In 1990, Cheryl Lau was elected Secretary of State, one of Nevada's highest offices.

Latin Americans have also played an important role in our state from its earliest discoveries. Spanish and Mexican traders traveled across our state on the way to California. In the mining era, there were many Latin-American workers in the silver and gold towns. They also were the victims of discrimination. Latin Americans worked on and owned ranches in Nevada during the early period of Nevada history. Today, Latin Americans serve in many prominent roles. In our legislature, Bob Coffin is a senator. Former Judge Mendoza is now chair of the state Public Service Commission. Manny Cortez was a county commis-

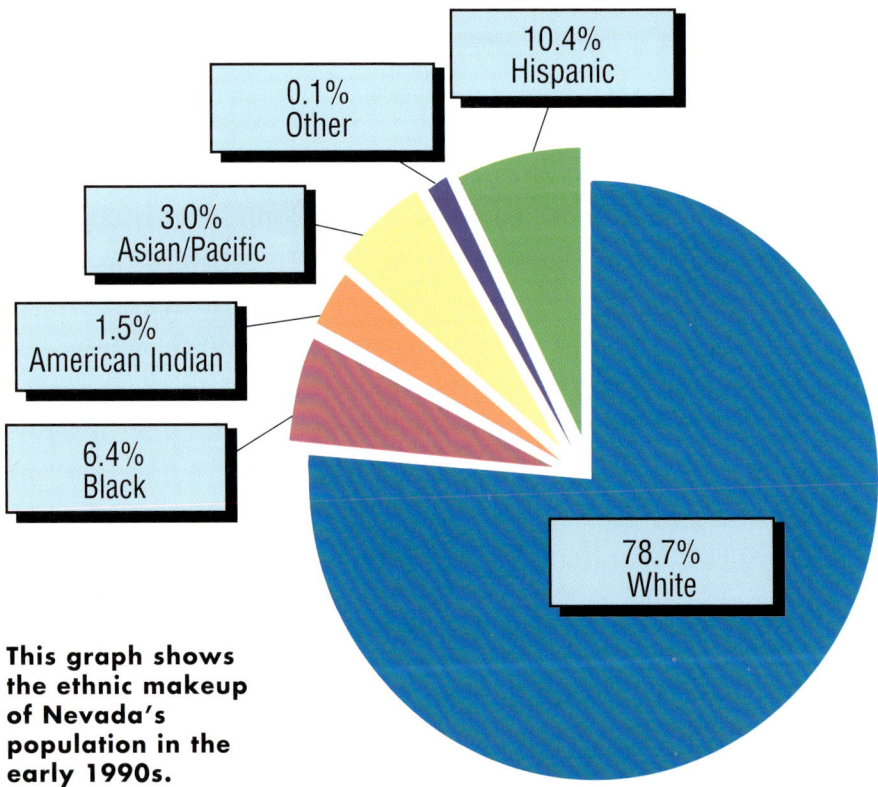

This graph shows the ethnic makeup of Nevada's population in the early 1990s.

sioner in Clark County and is now the head of the Convention Authority. Hispanics make up 10.4 percent of our state's population. They are a large and growing segment of our state.

All of these minorities have made important contributions to Nevada. Each group continues in their quest for equal treatment and justice.

Review Questions

1. What is the nickname for Nellis Air Force Base?
2. Describe the thunderbird in Indian legend.
3. What was stored around the town of Hawthorne?
4. Why were the factories in southern Nevada built?
5. What city was built near the factories?
6. Why was the Nevada Test Site built?

For Thought and Discussion

7. What else has been tested at the Nevada Test Site?
8. Why have so many military Bases been built in Nevada?
9. How did the building of the factories in Henderson help increase Nevada's population?
10. What happened at the Nevada Test Site that was dangerous to neighboring people?

Words to Know

dictator	industrial	stable
precision	ban	planetarium
depot	treaty	ethnic
extended family	fallout	independence
discrimination	rural	civil rights

Nevada's capitol is a good example of nineteenth-century architecture.

Chapter 10

NEVADA'S GOVERNMENT

Nevada has many levels of government. Each one affects the way we live. We live under laws of the United States government. We have a state government, county governments, and city governments.

Why We Need Government

An old prospector found a gold nugget at the edge of a river. Soon hundreds of people crowded the place looking for gold. Someone put up a sign that read "Get Rich, Nevada."

People hurriedly put up shacks, tents, and a few other buildings. There were no streets wide enough for a wagon. Outside every doorstep was thick mud. Because people threw their garbage out the backs of their houses, flies were thick when it was hot. People dumped waste matter into the river. They settled arguments in the town with

LEVELS OF GOVERNMENT

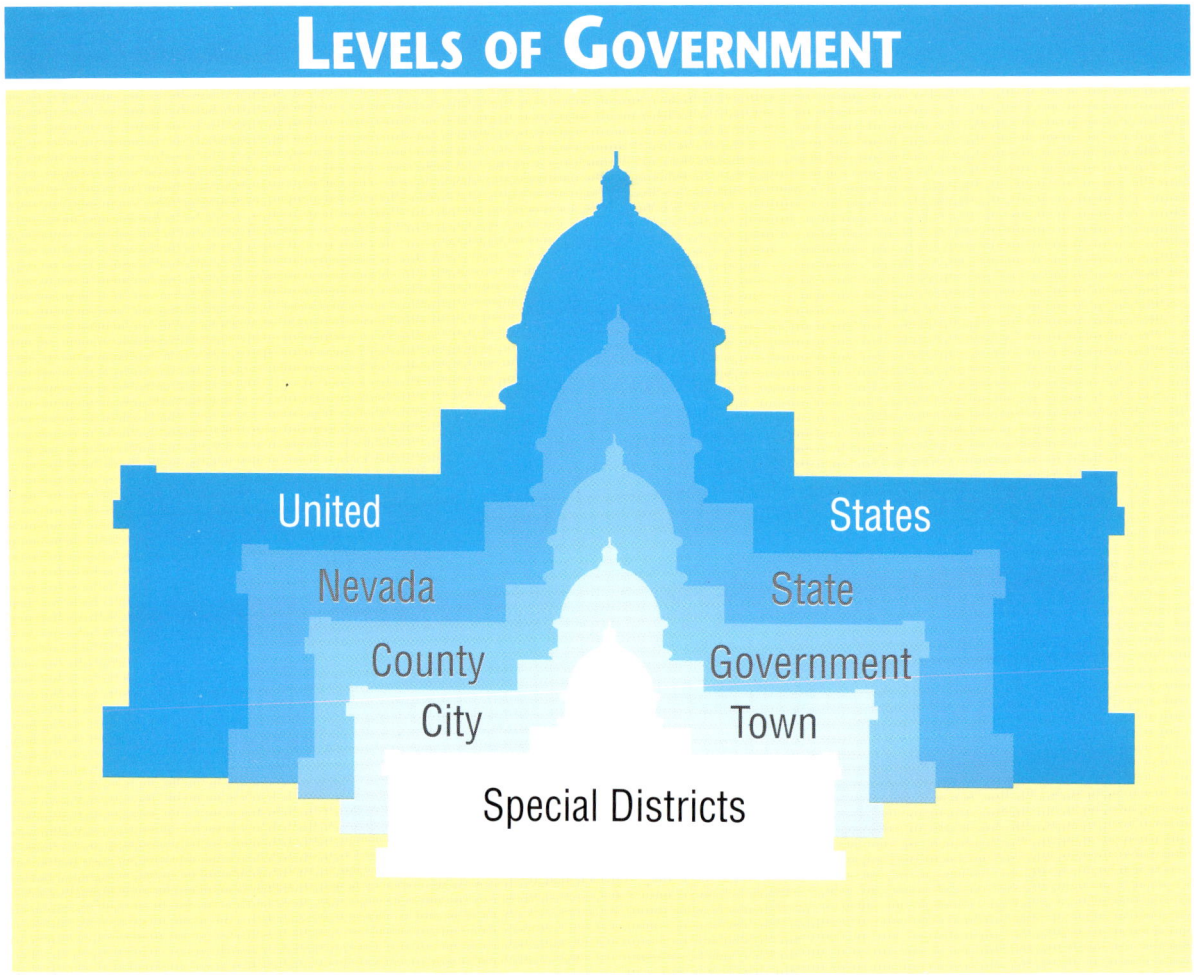

fists and guns, and the meanest people always got their way. They stole other people's gold. Nothing or no one was safe.

A few of the citizens in Get Rich have gotten together to decide what to do about their town. If you were part of the town meeting, what changes would you favor? What are the biggest problems that need attention? Would certain changes make Get Rich a better place to live?

The previous story shows how necessary governments are in our lives. Governments are responsible for making and **enforcing** laws and **regulations** for our citizens. These laws allow us to live in peace with our neighbors. Without these governments, our lives would be complete confusion.

Branches of Government

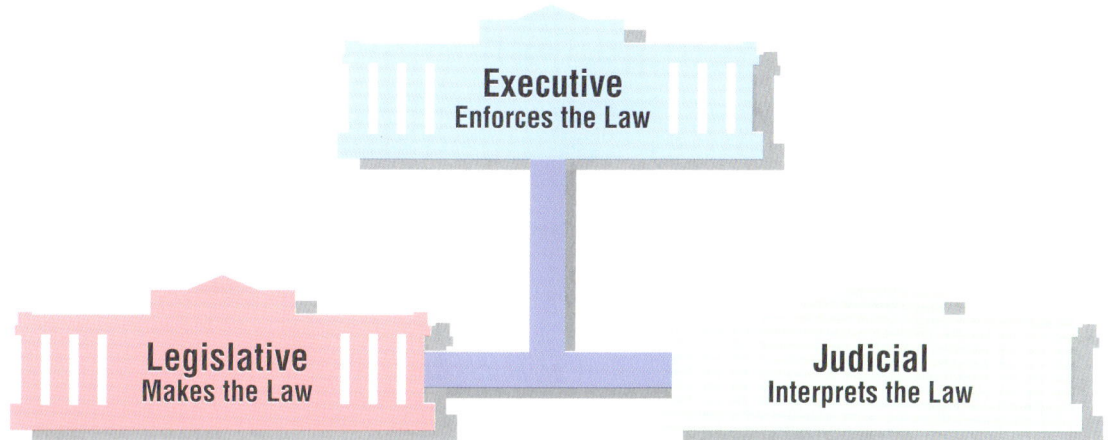

Branches of Government

Each level of government is divided into three **branches**, or parts. The **legislative** branch makes the laws. The **executive** branch carries out the laws. The **judicial** branch interprets the laws.

State Government

Nevada's state laws are made by two groups—the assembly and the senate. Together we call the assembly and the senate the **legislature**. There are 42 members of the assembly and 21 senators. Each represents a certain part of the state. Our government is based on the idea of one citizen, one vote. As a result, the places that have the most people have the most representatives. Reno and Las Vegas have the most representatives in the senate and the assembly because they have the largest populations. Some rural Nevadans dislike this system and feel they are not fairly represented.

The Nevada legislature meets once every two years at Carson City, the state's capital. The legislative session begins in January. Legislators meet to make the laws for our state. They also pass tax laws so the government will have the money it needs to carry out the laws.

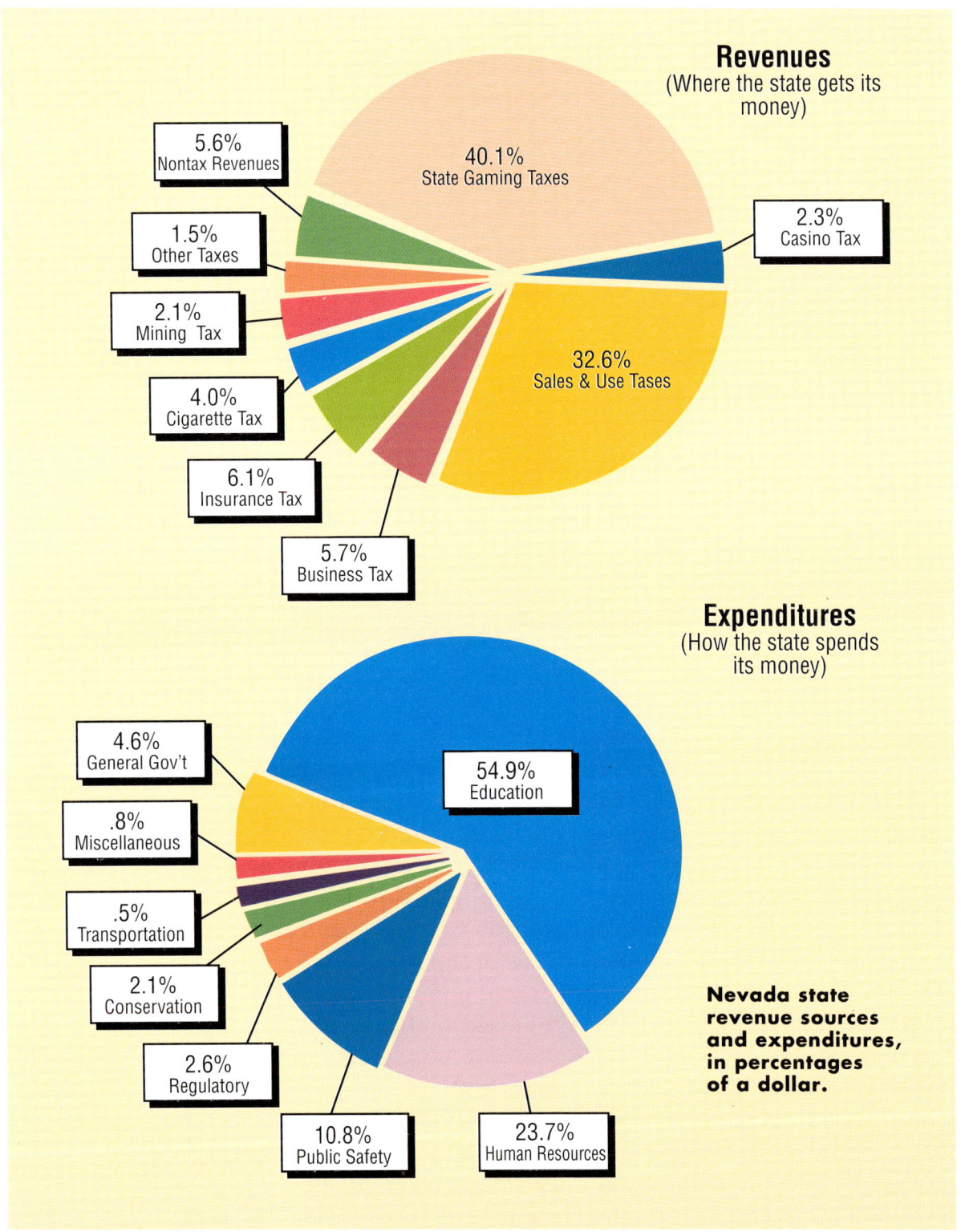

State Revenue & Expenditures

Revenues (Where the state gets its money)

- 40.1% State Gaming Taxes
- 5.6% Nontax Revenues
- 1.5% Other Taxes
- 2.1% Mining Tax
- 4.0% Cigarette Tax
- 6.1% Insurance Tax
- 5.7% Business Tax
- 32.6% Sales & Use Tases
- 2.3% Casino Tax

Expenditures (How the state spends its money)

- 54.9% Education
- 4.6% General Gov't
- .8% Miscellaneous
- .5% Transportation
- 2.1% Conservation
- 2.6% Regulatory
- 10.8% Public Safety
- 23.7% Human Resources

Nevada state revenue sources and expenditures, in percentages of a dollar.

Capitol Building

The state **capitol**, meaning the building, was begun in 1870 and finished by 1871. It was originally built for offices of both the governor and the legislature. But as the government became larger, the building became too small. Other buildings had to be constructed for the legislature. The original capitol is very beautiful. It contains marble from Alaska and windows of French crystal. It is one of the oldest buildings in Nevada. It is still used by the governor and his staff.

State Government Provides Many Services

The state government passes laws that affect everybody in Nevada. When you get your hair cut, the barber or beautician has to have a state license. Your dentist and doctor have to pass tests given by the state. Your teachers have to have a license to be in the classroom. Your house was built by workers such as carpenters, plumbers, and electricians who had to be licensed by the state. Why does the state require licenses? So that you can trust that these people are trained well enough to do a good job for you.

The state also provides many services for its citizens. There are agencies that provide for child **welfare** and help for the aged. There are an equal rights **commission** and a mental health division. Boxing and high school sports are regulated by the state. The state provides driver's licenses and sets up an historical society. There is a national guard for protection and a highway department to build our roads. All of the state government agencies are listed in the phone book. See how many you can find.

State Government Controls Gambling

In 1931, the state government legalized gambling in Nevada. At first, the government left it to the individual cities and counties to monitor casino businesses. As the gambling business grew, the state government took greater control of the casinos. The state wanted to make sure the casinos were run fairly so that tourists would continue to come to Nevada.

Public health workers are licensed by the state government.

This teacher is a licensed professional, who had to meet basic requirements to assure a quality education for her students.

How a Bill Becomes Law

All Nevada laws begin as bills. A bill is a written suggestion for a new law. The suggestion may come from any person in the state, but a bill must be presented to the legislature by one of its members. The bill is then sent to a committee. The committee holds hearings or discussions on it. Anyone can attend these hearings and present opinions on the bill.

After hearings and discussions, the legislature votes on the bill. If both houses approve the bill, it is sent to the governor. The governor may sign the bill into law, or the governor may **veto,** or reject, it. If a bill is vetoed, it fails to become law. The legislature can override the governor's veto. If two-thirds of the legislature vote again to pass the bill, it becomes law.

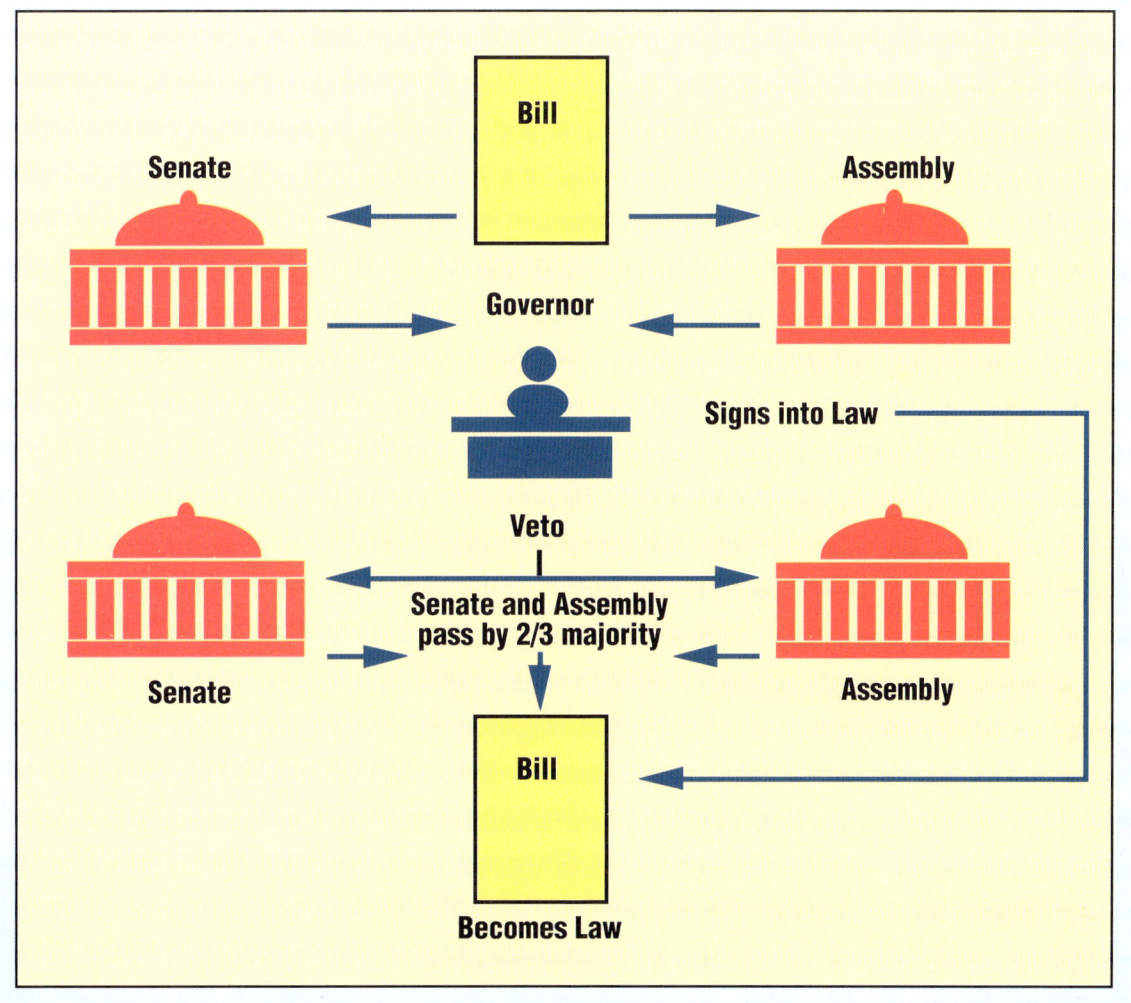

In the 1950s, the Nevada legislature created the Gaming Commission. It gave licenses to those who wanted to build, own, and work in casinos. It set rules for the casinos and collected taxes from them. The Gaming Control Board was also set up to help the commission carry out its rules. The Gaming Commission and the Gaming Control Board have overseen the gambling industry in Nevada for over 30 years. They have made sure that gambling is honest.

County Governments

County governments are responsible for keeping records of who owns land and the local taxes owed. They record births and deaths. They make county laws and hire sheriffs to enforce them. County laws concern issues such as pollution, the building of parks, and where houses, stores and other businesses can be built. County governments are important to our lives.

Nevada Counties

When Nevada became a territory in 1861, the territorial legislature created 9 counties. As more people moved into our state, they formed new counties. Today Nevada has 17 counties. Some were named after famous people. Others have very unusual names.

Lincoln County was named after one of our most famous presidents, Abraham Lincoln. He was president when Nevada became a state in 1864. Carson City County was named after the famous frontier scout Kit Carson. Clark County was named after Montana Senator Clark, who built the railroad through southern Nevada. Douglas County was named after U.S. Senator Stephen A. Douglas of Illinois. He had famous debates with Abraham Lincoln before Lincoln became president.

Some counties were named after natural features of our state. White Pine County was named for the many trees that grew in the area. Esmeralda gets its name from the Spanish word for emerald. Elko County has a name with Indian roots. Elko means beautiful. Mineral County is named for the many minerals found there.

Nevada's Counties

Eureka has a very unusual name. In Greek, *eureka* means "I have found it." Nevada miners were reported to have said this when they discovered silver and gold.

Six of our counties were named after famous military heroes. Ormsby and Storey were named for soldiers who died in the Pyramid Lake Indian War. Pershing, Lyon, Lander, and Churchill were all named for generals in the army.

Other famous people gave their names to our counties. Humboldt County was named after the river that passed through it. The river was named for a famous German scientist. Nye County was named for our first territorial governor, James W. Nye.

Native Americans lent their name to Washoe County. Some Nevadans even wanted to name our state Washoe.

Nevada even had a county in an area where practically no one lived. Bullfrog County was formed in 1987 in a section of Nye County. The county was organized to gain tax money from the federal government in case a nuclear dump was located there. The law forming the county was **repealed**, or done away with, in 1989.

City Governments

Nevada's cities also have governments. City government is concerned with helping and protecting people in that city. City governments hire the police department and the fire departments. They hire people to keep the streets clean and in good condition. City governments may provide services for water and the collecting of garbage. They also grant licenses to local businesses. If you have a dog, you buy its license from the city government.

A council and mayor are elected by the people to lead the city. Their job is to pass laws to keep the cities running smoothly. In some cities, a manager is hired to oversee the daily operations of the government.

Other Local Governments

Other local governments include school districts, health districts, library boards, and water districts. These governments make rules and provide services for the citizens of Nevada. Some of the people who serve on these boards are elected. Others are appointed by the city and county councils.

Local governments are able to be more responsive to the people's day-to-day needs than are state and national governments. This is because the local government officials and offices are closer to the people whom they serve. It is easier for government at this level to be in touch with what is going on in the communities each day.

All levels of government provide important services for the people.

It is our responsibility as citizens to be in touch with our government officials and let them know how we feel about issues that are being discussed. Once we are old enough to vote, we should do so. In these ways we are able to participate in government.

The city workers here and on page 156 are creating a park in Las Vegas.

Providing parks is one service a city performs. What are some others?

Questions for Review

1. Why are governments necessary?
2. Where does Nevada's legislature meet?
3. Who still meets in the old capitol?
4. What does the Nevada Gaming Commission do?
5. How many counties does Nevada have?
6. What president gave his name to a Nevada county?
7. Who runs the city governments in Nevada?

For Thought and Discussion

8. How does a bill become a law?
9. How did Nevada name its counties?
10. How do city governments help their residents?

Words to Know

enforce	executive	welfare
regulation	judicial	commission
branch	legislature	veto
legislative	capitol	repeal

Nevada's earliest American Indian people lived in harmony with their environment and made few changes. The pioneers found the environment difficult, but were unable to change it. Modern residents have changed their environment by bringing in water, electricity, and air conditioning. They have added comforts and entertainment. New York New York, shown here, is a mega-resort in Las Vegas.

Chapter 11

LIVING IN MODERN NEVADA

Nevada has become one of the fastest-growing states in the nation. Our favorable climate, recreation areas, small population, attractive living conditions, and wide-open spaces have brought thousands of new residents into Nevada. During the late 1980s, Reno was ranked in the top ten cities in America for its good living conditions. In 1989, Las Vegas was ranked 30th in *Money* magazine's "Best Places to Live in America" article. The growth of Las Vegas has made it one of the fastest-growing cities in our nation. In 1990, our capital, Carson City, was ranked as the nineteenth-best small city in the United States. And in 1993, Elko was named the best small town in the United States. Elko has 18,000 people, mining and gambling industries, an airport, and no debt. The town is also growing fast.

The rapid growth of population in Nevada has brought challenges. More roads and streets have to be built because more cars are using them. More schools will be needed. All of these things cost money.

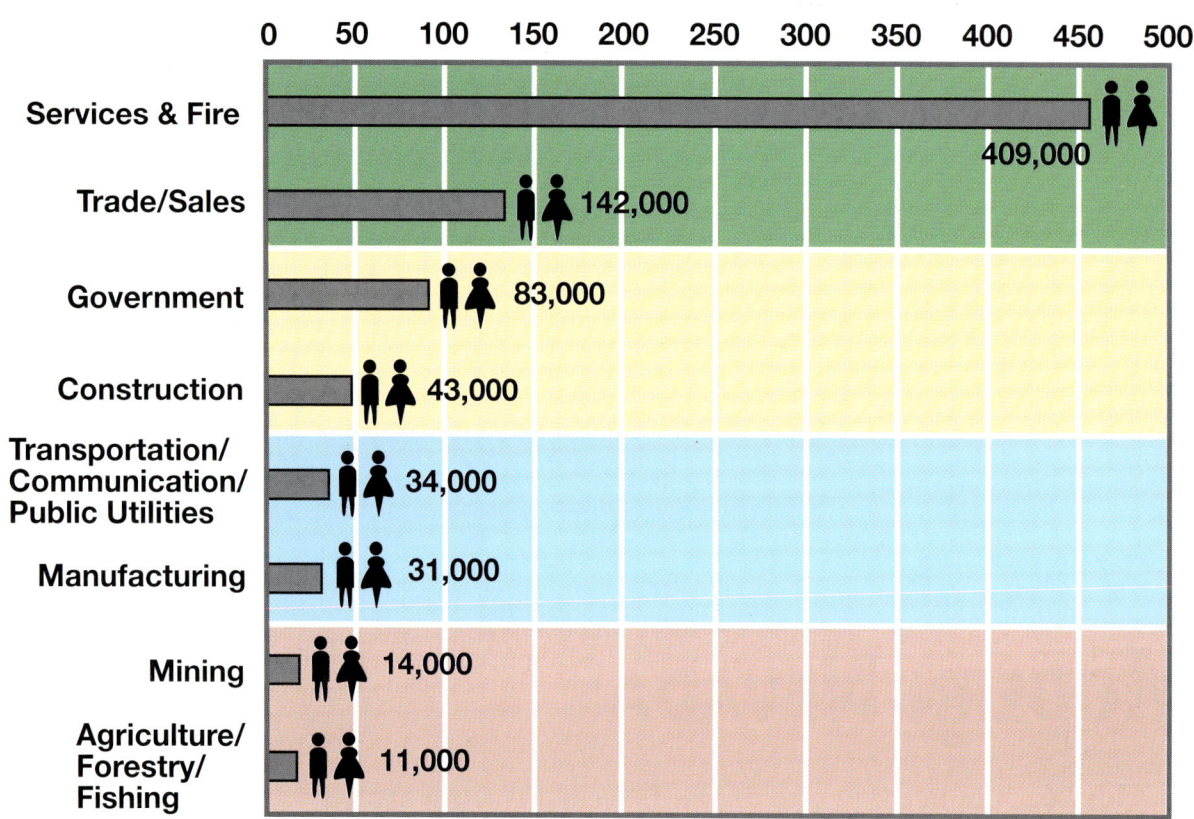

Home building has become big business as more people move here. Some new houses are being built in areas where wild animals used to live. This building is changing the ecology of our state. Desert tortoises, wild horses, and burros are being moved from their natural **habitats,** or homes, so more houses can be built. Some people are concerned about the future of these wild creatures.

Gambling, tourism, mining, ranching, farming, and industry have attracted many new people into our state too. While growth brings problems, it also brings progress and excitement. Young Nevadans will see the changes that growth brings.

Mega-Resorts—Nevada's New Trend

Nevada's pleasant climate and gambling casinos bring tourists to our state in great numbers. The 1960s, 1970s, and 1980s were decades that saw fantastic growth in our cities, with bigger and fancier hotels being built. The era of **mega-resorts** was beginning. A mega-resort is a very large resort. It may have one or more hotels, many casinos, and entertainment for all ages.

In Las Vegas, the Circus Circus, Hilton, MGM (Ballys), Mirage, and Excalibur resorts all have attracted families on vacation. In Reno, the Circus Circus, Hilton, MGM (Ballys), PepperMill and Fitzgeralds have done the same for northern Nevada. In the 1990s, theme park hotels have become popular. Treasure Island, Luxor, and the MGM Grand are the newest mega-resorts to attract tourists.

The small town of Laughlin became Nevada's newest resort area in the 1980s. Located on the Colorado River, across from the little town of Bullhead, Arizona, Laughlin was first known mostly by people who went there for the fishing. Then many new hotels and casinos were built. These gambling palaces attracted tourists from Arizona and California.

Modern Mining

Mining today is very different from that in the days of the prospectors. Today, **geologists**, or scientists who study minerals, explore areas that they think may contain minerals. If they find mineral deposits, then **engineers** go in. They build mills and plants to process the minerals. Huge trucks and diggers get the ore from the ground.

Mining is very important to Nevada's economy today. Many of the newest inventions in transportation, communication, electronics, engineering, and medicine use minerals that are found in Nevada. Copper, molybdenum, barite, mercury, diatomite, magnesia, perlite, gypsum, and fluorspar are minerals that have created a new bonanza in Nevada.

However, gold and silver still make the most money for mining companies. Since 1979, Nevada has been the number one gold-producing state in the nation. In 1988, Nevada again became the number one silver-producing state. In 1989, we produced over 5 million ounces of gold and almost 20 million ounces of silver.

Gold and silver are two of Nevada's most important minerals. This worker is pouring liquid gold.

Because mining companies make so much money from our minerals, the government is asking them to pay more taxes than before. Citizens are also demanding that mining companies take better care of the land they mine. When a mine is closed, the mining companies are now restoring the land to the way they found it. They level the land and plant native grasses and trees. The Amax Gold Company, which operates the Sleeper Mine in Humboldt County, even built ponds for birds and fish with water that they used in their mining.

Mining companies today try to improve the communities where their workers live. Some companies have built schools and recreation facilities in their towns.

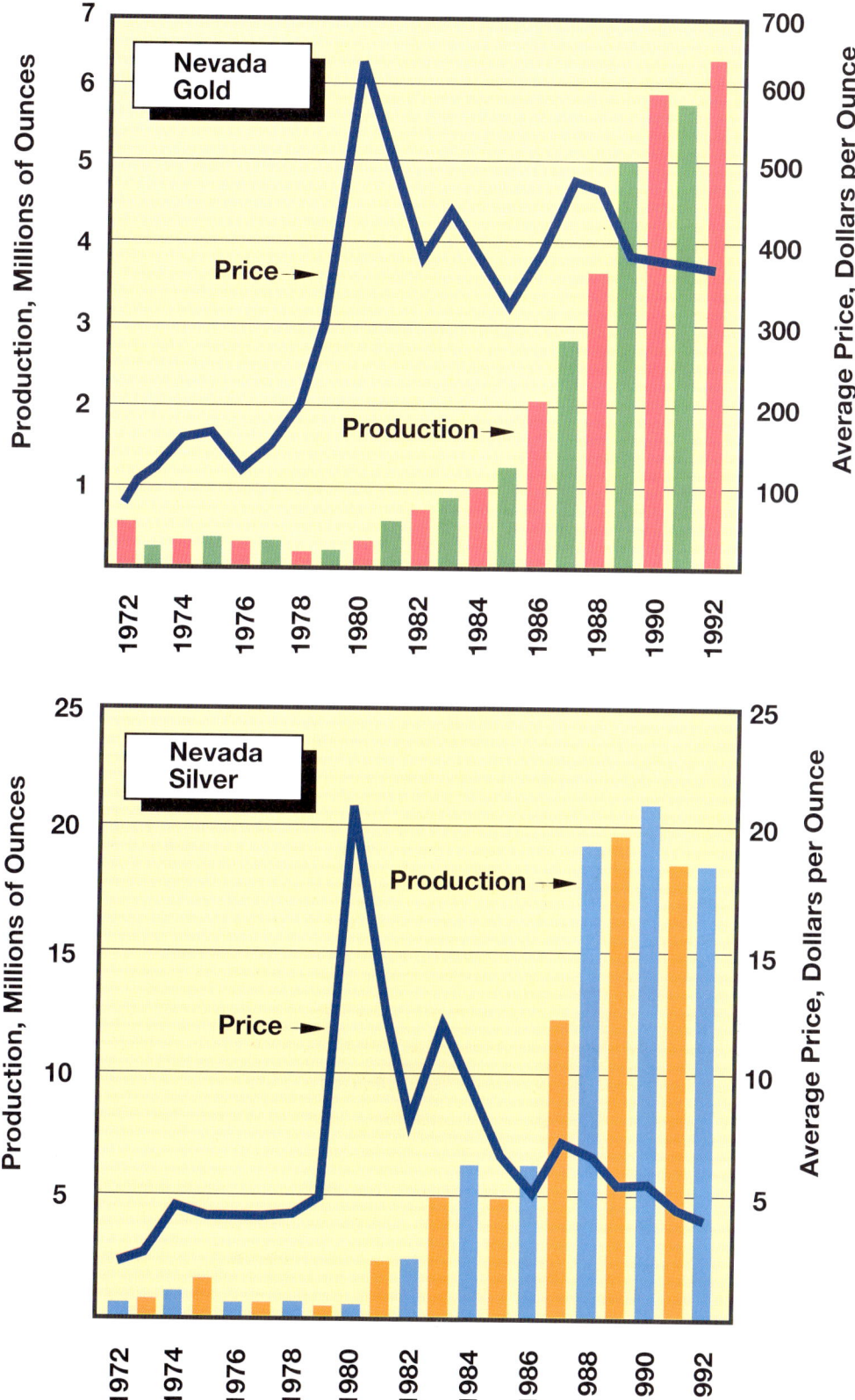

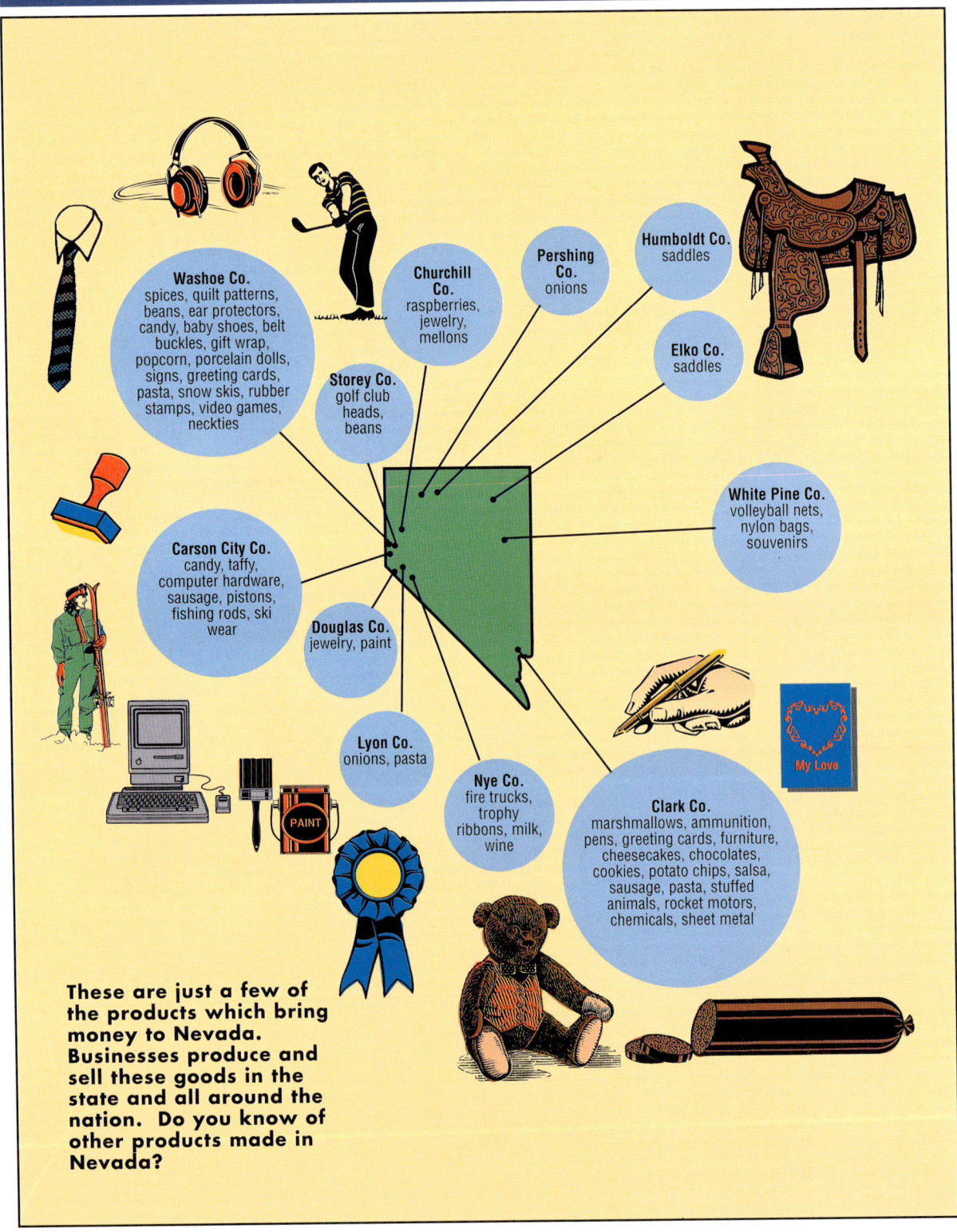

Industry Helps Nevada Progress

Henderson has been called the industrial center of Nevada. This city had the most industry in our state. From the mid-1900s, industries have helped Nevada grow.

The state legislature passed the Freeport Law in 1960. It allowed businesses to store and assemble merchandise to sell in other states, tax free. It attracted many industries to Nevada.

Manufacturing has also played a part in Nevada's growth. Manufacturers like Nevada because our state has low taxes and sufficient numbers of skilled workers to hire. Nevada businesses make ammunition in Boulder City, candy in Las Vegas, fire engines in Tonopah, gourmet spices in Sparks, golf-club heads in Dayton, and popcorn in Reno.

Because the hotel and casino business dominates Nevada's economy, most Nevadans work in jobs related to this industry. They work as janitors, maids, waiters, waitresses, salespeople, casino dealers, and cashiers.

Hotels hire companies to work on neon signs and air conditioners. Other workers build streets and maintain golf courses that both tourists and residents use.

Ranching and Farming

Ranching is still part of our economy today. Nevada has more than 1,700 ranches. Several of them are large, including the Russell Ranches near Eureka and the Ellison Ranching Company at Tuscarora.

However, most ranches are small, having 500 head of cattle or fewer. All of the ranches, big and small, lease land from the federal government. Their cattle eat the grass that grows on this land.

Farming is big business in many Nevada valleys. Moapa Valley, Carson Valley, and Smith Valley still produce farm items such as corn and dairy products. There is a winery in Pahrump that produces wine from home-grown grapes.

Challenges for the Future

Nevada's future is bright. Thousands of people move into our state every month. But growth brings many challenges and problems.

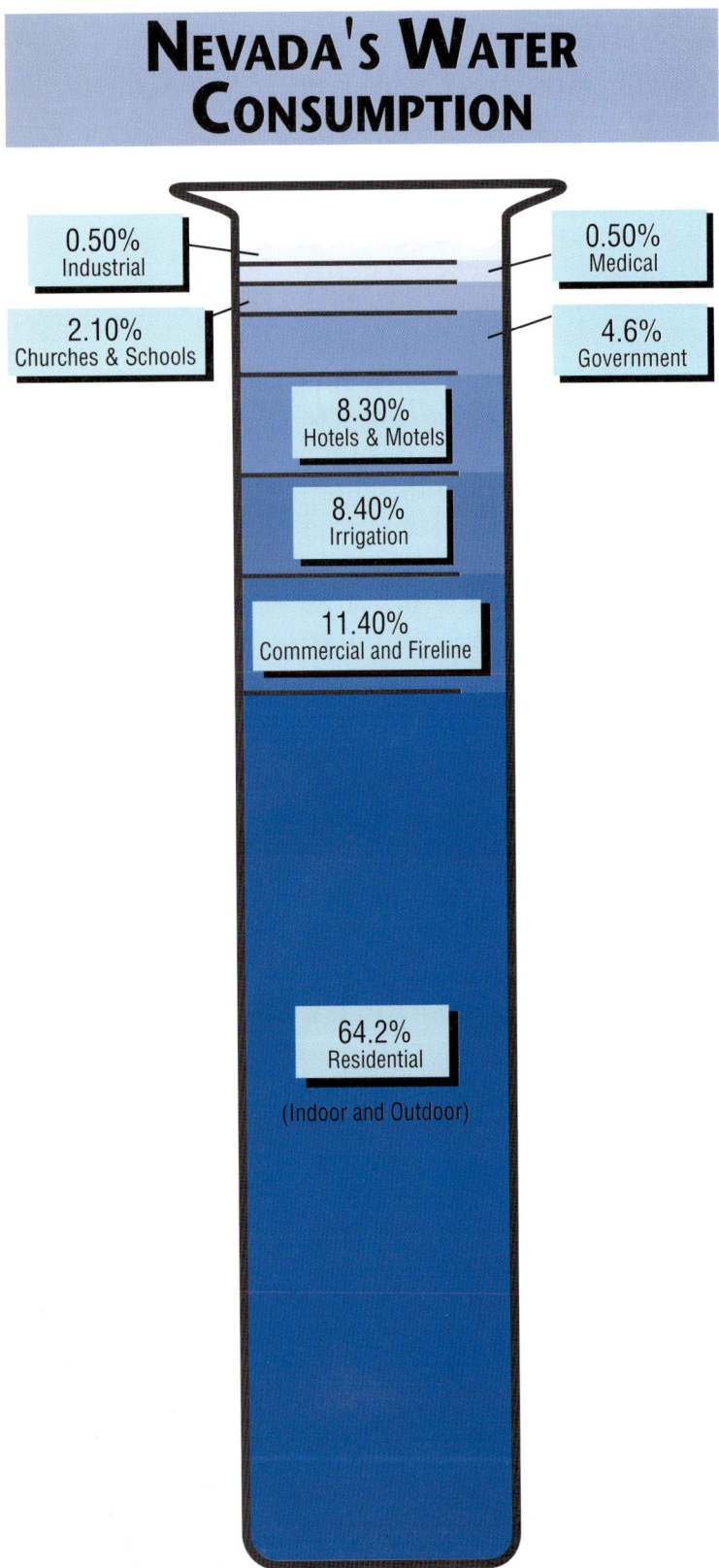

Water

One of the biggest challenges facing our state has to do with water. Southern Nevada receives 70 percent of its water from the Colorado River and Lake Mead. With thousands of people moving to this area each year, the demand for water grows. The local governments are now planning to control water usage so that we will have enough of this precious fluid in the future.

However, many people who moved here came from areas of the country with lakes and rivers. These people like their homes near water. Some home builders have built artificial lakes in new subdivisions. This is an advantage for residents. But such lakes could create problems in a desert environment. Can you think what some of the problems might be? Can you think of some ways to solve the problems?

In northern Nevada, the water issue is not related just to population growth. The area is sometimes hit by a **drought,** or long period of dryness. This lack of rain and snow causes the level of water in the Walker and Truckee rivers to fall. Many farmers and ranchers then have to stop farming. Drought also limits the number of people who can move into this area.

This is spring runoff at Lamoille Creek, in the Ruby Mountains. Having enough water is important to our modern living. What part does nature play in our water supply?

Nuclear Waste Repository

Another problem that Nevada faces is **nuclear waste.** High-level nuclear waste is the remains of atomic material that is used in producing such things as atomic-powered submarine fuel. Nuclear power plants also produce nuclear waste when they make electricity. Nuclear waste is still very dangerous material. It must be stored safely where it will not affect the people and other living things. Nevada has been chosen by the federal government as a possible storage place for the nation's nuclear waste. We have a small population, and our state is large. There are many wide-open spaces where no one lives.

The federal government believes the **repository** would not harm anyone. Since we have already allowed atomic testing in Nevada, officials don't see why we would be opposed to a nuclear dump. The government has paid for many ads in the newspapers and on television. The ads attempt to show the safety of moving nuclear waste on our highways to a nuclear repository in our state.

Many people who oppose the nuclear dump believe there could be accidents while moving the nuclear waste into Nevada. They also believe that the dangers of nuclear waste could keep tourists from visiting our state.

Nevada has many interesting challenges ahead. Nevada's young people will lead the state in meeting these changes. You and your classmates will have the opportunity to make our state better. What you learn in school today will help you become the leaders of tomorrow.

Review Questions

1. Why are many people moving to Nevada today?
2. What is a mega-resort?
3. Name some of the new mega-resorts.
4. What is the newest resort gambling town in Nevada?
5. What minerals bring the most money to Nevada today?
6. Name some of the things made in Nevada.
7. Name two large ranches in Nevada.
8. What is a nuclear waste repository?

For Thought and Discussion

9. How is mining today different from that of the past?
10. What problems does Nevada face today in the areas of water, nuclear waste, and population growth?

Words to Know

habitat
mega-resort
geologist
engineer
nuclear waste
repository

Glossary

ability: a skill, natural talent

adapt: to do things differently in order to get along in a new situation or a new place; to adjust

adopt: to make something one's own; to start using a new thing

archaeologist (ar-kee-ALL-uh-jist): a scientist who studies the life of people from long ago

artesian well (ar-TEE-zhun): a deep-bored well from which water flows like a fountain

artifact (AR-ti-fakt): an object made by people long ago

autobiography (AH-tow-by-OG-ruh-fee): the story of a person's life written by himself or herself

ban: an official order to stop something

basin: a wide, mostly flat valley surrounded by higher land; the land drained by a river

bill: a written idea for a new law

blown out of proportion: made to sound worse than what really happened

bonanza: a rich ore field found by miners

branch: one of the three main parts of government

bullion (BULL-yun): bars of gold or silver metal

carnivore (CAR-nih-vore): an animal that eats meat

civil rights: freedoms guarded by law for all people of a nation

claim *n*.: a piece of land lawfully staked out as a miner's property

climate: the weather pattern of an area over many years

commission: a group given orders to perform certain duties

continent: one of the seven large land areas of the world

convert *v*. (kun-VERT): to change a person's beliefs or ideas

county seat: the city where government offices of the county are located

culture (KUL-cher): the way of life of a group of people—their food, clothing, houses, art, music, religion

customs: the way a group of people usually do things

depot (DEE-poh): a place where military supplies are kept

destination: a place that is set for the end of a journey

dictator: a person who rules a country with total power

discriminate (dis-KRIM-ih-nait): to treat some people worse than others

discrimination (dis-krim-ih-NAI-shun): treating people unjustly because they are different

document: a paper written to give facts or proof

drifter: a person who moves around to find work

drought (drowt): a long period of dry weather

economy (ee-KON-uh-mee): the way a country takes care of its money

elevation: the height of the land above sea level

emigrant (EHM-uh-grunt): a person who leaves home to settle somewhere else far away; the opposite of *immigrant*

endangered species: the last of a group of animals or plants that might die off

enforce: to make certain that laws and rules are followed

engineer: a person who plans and builds something

environment (en-VY-run-munt): the surroundings people live in

erode: to wear away the land by wind or water

ethnic: said of races or people from other countries with common traits and customs

executive: the person in charge of a government; the one who puts laws into action

explorer: a person who goes into a new area to learn about it

extended family: a large group of related people living together, usually with grandparents and some aunts, uncles, and cousins

fallout: harmful dust and sand produced by atomic bombs

fossil: the print or remains of a plant or animal left long ago in soil or rock

geography: the study of the earth and the people, animals, and plants living on it

geologist (jee-AHL-uh-jist): a scientist who studies minerals and rocks

grubstake: to give a prospector supplies or money for his promise to share the gold or silver

habitat: the place where a plant or animal usually lives

hard-rock mining: digging gold, silver, or other minerals from rocks deep within the earth

harsh: hard, trying, unpleasant

hemisphere (HEM-iss-feer): half of the earth

historic: said of people who kept written records

immigrant (IHM-uh-grunt): a person who comes to

live here from another country; the opposite of *emigrant*

independence: freedom from control or rule by someone else

industrial: said of an area with many factories

irrigation: a way of supplying water to dry land through ditches, canals, or pipes

judicial (joo-DIH-shul): having to do with courts and judges who interpret the laws

landform: a shape formed on the earth's surface by nature, such as a hill, a cave, or a valley

latitude (LA-tih-tood): the distance on a map north or south of the equator, measured in degrees

lease: to rent the use of land for a period of time

legend: a story passed down through the ages

legislative (LEH-jus-lai-tiv): having to do with making or passing laws

legislature (LEH-jus-lai-chur): a group of people having the power to make or change laws

longitude (LON-jih-tood): the distance on a map east or west of a zero line drawn between the north and south poles, measured in degrees

mega-resort (MEG-uh ree-zort) a very large vacation place with hotel(s), games, and live shows

meridian: another name for a longitude line on a map

movement: the motion of news, goods, or people from one place to another

navigation (nav-ih-GAI-shun): traveling by water

nuclear waste (NEW-klee-ur): the harmful remains from atomic power

obstacle: something that stands in the way

ore: a rock containing gold, silver, or some other mineral

outcropping: bits of gold, silver, or some other mineral sticking above the ground; a clue for where to dig a mine

pelt: the skin of an animal with the fur on

petroglyph (PET-roh-glif): a carving left on rocks by people long ago

pithouse: a home built partly underground by the Anasazi people, entered through the roof

placer mining: picking up loose rocks and washing them to find bits of gold or silver

planetarium (PLAN-eh-TAIR-ee-um): a building that shows pictures of the stars and planets on the ceiling

precious: said of a rare and high-priced gem

precipitation: rain, snow, hail, or sleet falling to the earth; a source of water

precision: being very exact and flawless in motion

prehistoric: from a time before written records were kept

prey: victims of meat-eating animals

region: an area where the land looks mostly the same (such as a desert region); or an area where people do mostly the same kind of work with the land (such as a farming region)

register: to enter one's name on a list

regulation: a rule or an order from a government

rendezvous (RON-dai-voo): a planned meeting, usually for mountain men to sell their furs

repeal: to do away with a law

repository: a place where harmful wastes are stored

reservation: in the 1860s, a new section of land where the U.S. government forced a whole Native American tribe to live

reservoir (REZ-er-vwahr): a machine-made lake for storing water

ruin: something still left of the homes of people from long ago

rural: said of farm areas or country life

semi-precious: said of gems easier to find and lower in price than precious gems

smelt: to melt the metal out of ore rocks

stable: showing little or no change

staple: a main food

stock: farm animals raised for sale

suffrage: the right to vote

symbol: a thing that stands for something else; a plant, animal, or mineral that stands for Nevada

territorial government: the system for voting and making laws before an area becomes a state

thermal: caused by heating within the earth

trade *n*: the buying and selling of goods

trader: a person who sells goods and supplies; or a person who gives some supplies and takes other supplies instead of money

transcontinental (TRANS-kon-tih-NEN-tul): crossing the United States from the Atlantic Coast to the Pacific Coast

treaty: an agreement between two or more countries to do or stop doing something

trestle (TRES-ul): the frame under a bridge where trains cross a canyon

tribe: a large group of similar people

urban: said of city areas

vein: a deposit of minerals in the ground

veto: to reject, to refuse to sign a bill into law

wagon train: several pioneer families traveling together, being pulled in wagons

welfare: help, aid, relief, security, protection of children

Acknowledgements and Photo Credits

The author wishes to thank the many people who assisted in the making of this book and extends appreciation to the following people and organizations who provided photographs, artwork, and current data.

Letters beside the numbers designate position on the page: T (top), M (middle), B (bottom), L (left), R (right).

Arizona Historical Society, 96

Gary BeDunnah, 35

Phil Beemer, 137

Larry Benham, 3, 4

Donn Blake, Courtesy City of Las Vegas, 155, 156

Bureau of the Census, 142

Chicago Historical Society, 99

Clark County Heritage Museum, 135T

Courtesy of Doris Clymer, 50, 55, 57

Frontier Printing, 65

John P. George, © v, 10, 24, 25, 39, 167

The Grace Dangberg Foundation, resource maps

Hearns Brothers Map, 40, 43

Lake Mead National Recreation Area, 5, 6, 26, 94

Las Vegas News Bureau, 124, 158

Las Vegas Review-Journal, 164

Las Vegas Sun, 166

Cheryl A. Lau, 141TR

Shirley McLees, 150B

Helen Myers, Nevada State Office of Small Business, 164

Nellis Air Force Base, 130

Nevada Commission on Tourism, 8

Nevada Department of Minerals, 7, 9, 108, 144, 163

Nevada Department of Transportation, resource maps

Nevada Historical Society, 45, 46, 75, 117

Nevada Legislative Counsel Bureau, 2, 140, 141TL, 148

Nevada State Occupational Information Committee, 160

Northeastern Nevada Museum, 38, 74, 76, 79, 84, 85, 89, 98B 102, 104, 105, 106, 112, 120, 126, 139

Reno News Bureau, 29, 127TL

Thomas J. Sanker, 23, 42

Madelyn Suttles, 162

Tom Till, © 20, 21, 22, 32, 66

United States Bureau of Reclamation, photo by E. Hertzog, 123

University of Nevada Las Vegas, 119, 122, 135B

University of Nevada Reno, 90

University of Oklahoma, 103

University of Washington Libraries, Special Collections Division, Asahel Curtis photo #19943, 100

Utah State Historical Society, 41, 44, 52, 53, 54, 58, 59, 62, 64, 67, 68, 72, 87, 98T 116

Jeannie Young, 110, 127BR, 150T

INDEX

Abbott, William E., 102
Adams, Jewett W., 101
African Americans, 58, 103, 134, 141
Air bases, 130–133
Altube, Pedro, 104
Anasazi Indians, 34–36
Animals, 5–6, 8, 10, 24–26, 39–40, 53–54, 88
Arberry, Morse, 141
Artifacts, 33
Asian Americans, 141–142
Atomic bomb test sites, 136–137
Automobiles, 112, 116–117
Basques, 104–106
Beaver, 53–54
Beckwourth, James, 58
Bidwell-Bartelson Party, 69, 71
Boulder City, 124
Browne, J. Ross, 78
Camels, 88
Capitol, 144, 149
Carson City, 84, 90
Central Pacific Railroad, 106
Chinese, 86, 139
Civil War 1, 3, 90, 103
Clark, William, 118
Coffin, Bob, 141
Colorado River, 95, 123
Commission on Equal Rights of Citizens, 141
Comstock Lode, 77, 80, 82, 116
Cotton, 95
Counties, 152–154
Cowboys, 101–103
Dangberg, Fred, 101
Dat-so-la-lee, 45–46
Deidesheimer, Philipp, 81
DeQuille, Dan, 79, 81–82

Desert, 67–68, 72, 88
Divorce law, 128
Donner Party, 67
Electricity, 116, 123–124, 134
Elko, 159
Environment, 27, 137–138, 162, 168
Equator, 15–16
Ethnic minorities, 139, 143
Executive branch of government, 147, 151
Fitzpatrick, Thomas "Broken Hand," 69
Fallout, 137–138
Farming and ranching, 35, 43, 63, 93–98, 101–108, 110, 120, 160, 165
Ferris wheel, 99
Fong, Lilly, 142
Forty-Mile Desert, 67
Fremont, John C., 59–60
Gambling, 29, 125–128, 149, 152, 160
Gans, Joe 115
Gemstones, 8–9
Geography, 14
Government, 90, 145–155
Great Basin, 30, 36, 59
Great Depression, 121–122, 131
Great Salt lake, 71
Greenwich, England, 16
Hawthorne ammunition depot, 133
Helldorado, 126
Henderson, 134–135
Highways, 117, 125
Hillyer, C.J., 100, 113
Hispanics, *see Latin Americans*
Homestead Act of 1862, 96
Hoover Dam, 36, 96, 122–124, 126, 134
Ichthyosaur, 7, 18
Indians, *see Native Americans*
Industry, 160, 164–165
Japanese, 139
Judicial branch of government, 147

Knight, Amelia, 66
Lahontan Dam, 121
Lake Lahontan, 19–20, 33
Lake Mead, 36, 96, 123
Lake Tahoe, 127–128
Lakes, 8, 19–20, 33, 36, 96, 123, 127–128
Landforms, 19, 21
Las Vegas, 27, 59, 119, 122, 132, 134–135, 137, 159
Las Vegas School, 120
Latin Americans, 120, 139, 141–142
Latitude, 15
Lau, Cheryl A., 141
Legislative branch of government, 147, 151
Leonard, Zenas, 58
Longitude, 15–16
Love, Nat, 103
Lovelock Cave people, 33–36
Manly, Lewis, 71
Martin, Anne, 113
Mason, H.N.A., 101
McGill, William N., 101
Mega-resorts, 158, 160–161
Mendoza, Judge, 142
Mining, 7, 29, 36, 72–90, 94–95, 110, 114–116, 119, 134, 145, 160–163
Mississippi River, 63
Mormon Fort, 92, 94, 120
Mormon Station, 75, 92
Mountain men, 50, 54–57, 60, 63, 69, 71, 73.
Native Americans, 6, 24, 27, 37–48, 55–56, 65–66, 140
Neal, Joe, 141
Neighboring states, 15–16, 28, 34, 51–52, 59
Nellis Air Force Base, 130, 132
Nelson, "Battling," 115
Nevada Central Railroad, 108
Newlands, Senator Francis, 121
North America, 15
Nuclear waste, 168
Ogden, Peter Skene, 57
Old Spanish Trail, 59, 71, 94
Pacific Ocean, 22–23, 126
Pearl Harbor, 131
Petroglyphs, 32, 34
Pine nuts, 37–39
Pioche and Bullionville Railroad, 108
Pioneers, 24, 28, 58, 64–73, 89, 94–95
Plate tectonics, 18–19
Pony Express, 86–87
President Buchanan, 90
President Abraham Lincoln, 1, 90, 152
Ptolemy, 15
Pueblo Grande, 35–36
Rabbits, 39–40
Raffetto, Bertha, 5
Railroads, 84, 95–96, 106–109, 118
Reed, James Frazier, 67
Reed, Margaret, 67
Reed, Virginia, 68
Reno, 27, 127, 159
Reservations, 47
Riverboats, 95–96
Rivers, 8, 34, 59, 67–68, 71–72, 76, 96, 121
Rocky Mountains, 47
Rudd, Lydia, 69
Rye Patch Dam, 121
Sagebrush, v, 5, 24, 104
San Pedro, Los Angeles and Salt Lake Railroad, 118
San Buenaventura, 52
Sandstone, 8–9
Scott, Eddie, 141
Shadow effect, 23
Siegel, Benjamin "Bugsy," 125

Sierra Nevada, 22–23, 47, 75
Smith, Jedediah Strong, 56–57
Smith, Raymond "Pappy," 126
Spanish priests, 51–52
Sparks, John, 101
Square-set cribs, 80–81
State flag, 3
State seal, 1
Stevens-Murphy-Townsend Party, 71
Stewart, Helen J., 94, 119
Stewart, Archibald, 94
Sutro tunnel, 82
Territorial government, 90
Thunderbird flying team, 130–133
Tourism, 29, 31, 125, 127–128, 160
Traders, 51, 53
Trails, 76
Transcontinental railroad, 106
Trestles, 84–85
Truckee-Carson Irrigation Project, 121

Twain, Mark, 2, 82–83
United States government, 47, 145, 168
University of Nevada at Reno, 138
University of Nevada, Las Vegas, 138
Utah Territory, 89, 92
Virginia and Truckee Railroad, 108
Virginia City, 78–79, 82, 84, 88–89
Wagon trains, 62, 64–65, 69, 71
Walker, Joseph, 58
Washington, D.C., 45
Water, 17, 28, 34–35, 96, 121, 123, 125, 166–167
Williams, Wendell, 140
Wilson, Woodrow, 141
Winnemucca, Sarah, 45
Women's rights, 100, 113
Wootton, Richens "Uncle Dick, 103
World War I, 120
World War II, 126, 131–132, 138–140
Young, Brigham, 89–90, 92, 94